AF422406

Lord, Please Help Me

GOD'S TRUTH & LIGHT FOR DARK TIMES

30-DAY DEVOTIONAL

DR. O'SHEA LOWERY

Published by Innovo Publishing, LLC
www.innovopublishing.com
1-888-546-2111

Innovo Publishing LLC is a Christ-centered publisher located near Memphis, TN. Since 2008, Innovo has published quality books, eBooks, audiobooks, music, screenplays, and online and physical curricula that support the Great Commission, equip believers, and help create a positive Christian worldview. Innovo's capabilities and global reach provide Christian authors, artists, and ministries access to the world for Christ. To learn more about Innovo Publishing, visit our website at innovopublishing.com. To connect with other Christian creatives and to learn best practices for creating, publishing, marketing, and selling Christian titles, visit the Christian Publishing Portal at cpportal.com.

LORD, PLEASE HELP ME
God's Truth & Light for Dark Times

Library of Congress Control Number: 2024950418
ISBN: 979-8-88928-061-3

Cover Design & Interior Layout: Innovo Publishing, LLC

Printed in the United States of America
U.S. Printing History
First Edition: 2024

I would like to dedicate this book to my mother, Patricia Ann Quinn.

For years, my mother cheered me on in my writing career before it ever came to realization. Her continual message to me was, "One day." One day, this will happen. In eras when I was weary from my journey, my mother encouraged me to keep going and to keep believing that one day my dream of being a writer would come to fruition. I am thankful not only for my mother's belief in me but also for her wisdom imparted to me, her life lessons entrusted to me, and her unconditional love for me. Thank you, Momma!

Contents

-Day 1-
He's Holding You 9

-Day 2-
Open My Eyes to See the Yellow Flowers 12

-Day 3-
Standing on the Other Side of Our Dreams 15

-Day 4-
A Heart That Is Wounded Cries Loudly Through Actions 18

-Day 5-
For Such a Time as This, You Have Been Placed and Positioned 21

-Day 6-
Balcony People vs. Basement People 26

-Day 7-
The Courage to Bring Our Past to Christ 30

-Day 8-
Just When You Think It's Over, Suddenly. 34

-Day 9-
Waiting Times: Eyes in the Sky vs. the Sideline View 37

-Day 10-
Prepare Your Chariot 41

-Day 11-
It's Not About the Masses; It's About the One 45

-Day 12-
Let God Seat You 50

-Day 13-
A Desolate Situation Met by a Savior 54

-Day 14-
Look at the Lesson, Not the Offense 58

-Day 15-
What Is Holding Your Attention? 62

-Day 16-
Though None Go With Me 66

-Day 17-
Who Is Standing at Your Sideline? 70

-Day 18-
Journeying On, Continuing Toward 74

-Day 19-
How to Deal Biblically with the Trial at Hand 78

-Day 20-
Be Careful with Counsel from Others...82

-Day 21-
The Portion of the Field 86

-Day 22-
Please Stay on the Wall; Someone Needs You.................................91

-Day 23-
On the Other Side of God's Call to Go..95

-Day 24-
What to Do When We Don't Know What to Do 99

-Day 25-
Prayer: The Greatest Tool We Have 104

-Day 26-
But the Nine—Where Are They?...108

-Day 27-
A Troubled Soul Met by a Faithful Savior.................................112

-Day 28-
"What Do You Want Me to Do for You?" 116

-Day 29-
Even if You Let Go of Me, I Will Not Let Go of You....................120

-Day 30-
What Then Do You Say, Lord?...124

More from Dr. O'Shea Lowery & Innovo Publishing........................129

"Do not fear, for I am with you;
Do not anxiously look about you, for I am your God.
I will strengthen you, surely I will help you,
Surely I will uphold you with My righteous right hand."
—Isaiah 41:10

Have you ever heard the expression, "A picture speaks a thousand words"? I have, and I know with certainty that it is true. It is also accurate that a picture can voice a message of truth, which can remind a weary soul—or even a fearful one—that God is with them no matter what He is calling them to do or what they may be going through.

Over the past several months, God has been speaking to me, confirming it is time for me to *step out* and move forward to something He is calling me to do. I will be honest, as exciting as the call is, I have been somewhat fearful of moving forward.

This past week, my son, daughter-in-law, and grandkids took a vacation at the beach. As I received pictures from the trip, I began to view each one. A smile swept over my face as I looked through the pictures of my family and their beautiful surroundings. Yet one particular photo gripped my heart like no other. The message it portrayed touched my life in a way I had not expected.

The picture was of a mother holding her son as he looked beyond the shoreline to the beautiful ocean, taking in the gorgeous sunset. As I stared at the picture, God again reminded my heart that no matter what He calls me to do, He will be with me every step of the way. Just like my daughter-in-law held my grandchild as he looked beyond the horizon from where he was standing, my heavenly Father will hold me as well and will never leave me.

No matter what we are facing, God is holding us, loving us, and giving us the grace to put one foot in front of the other. You are going to be more than just *OK*. You are His child. He is holding you.

To those whom God is calling to do something new, you do not have to fear. You can confidently step out of the boat and do the thing He is asking you to do. You do not have to just look at the horizon—you can actually move *toward* it. He is holding you.

> *Peter said to Him, "Lord, if it is You, command*
> *me to come to You on the water." And He*
> *said, "Come!" And Peter got out of the boat, and*
> *walked on the water and came toward Jesus.*
> *(Matthew 14:28-29)*

To those whom God has redirected their journey, He is calling you to trust Him and to be at rest in Him. Instead of pondering on the past, reflecting on how things used to be, God is calling you to move forward with Him to the future He has waiting for you.

> *"Do not call to mind the former things,*
> *Or ponder things of the past.*
> *Behold, I will do something new,*
> *Now it will spring forth;*

> *Will you not be aware of it?*
> *I will even make a roadway in the wilderness,*
> *Rivers in the desert."*
> *(Isaiah 43:18-19)*

No matter what God is doing in your life, remember: He is holding you. No matter what you are currently facing, remember: He is holding you. And no matter what He is calling you to do, remember: He is holding you. My friend, look beyond your shoreline to the horizon that is awaiting. He is holding you.

Lord, please help me . . .

____

____

____

____

____

____

____

Then God opened her eyes and she saw a well of water; and she went and filled the skin with water and gave the lad a drink.
—*Genesis 21:19*

That Saturday was normal, just like any other. However, the ground was messy from stormy weather and heavy rains. I was visiting with family back in Alabama and was standing outside by the door to my mother's home, awaiting entrance, when my eyes caught a glimpse of some tall, yellow flowers in the middle of a watery yard. I had never noticed such flowers on my mother's lawn prior to this day. Yet amidst a soggy yard, there they stood, tall and lovely in the middle of a wet and dreary day.

As I continued staring at the beautiful flowers, a great truth tugged at my heart. If we will just take the time to notice, God brings beauty out of seemingly messy places. While we may find ourselves focusing on what appears to be a fragmented and hopeless situation, God is opening a flower bud of miracles and blessings, ordained before the beginning of time.

Hagar had been cast out of her home by a family she had loved and served. She was rejected and mistreated, while bearing a wound that bore great anguish. For a time, a desert became the new dwelling place for Hagar and her son. She felt alone, scared, and uncertain of her future. Due to the scarcity of water, Hagar thought certainly she and her son would die, for all she could see was desert and desolation. Yet, unbeknownst to Hagar, God had a plan.

> *Abraham rose early in the morning and took bread and a skin of water and gave them to Hagar, putting them on her shoulder, and gave her the boy, and sent her away. And she departed and wandered about in the wilderness of Beersheba. When the water in the skin was used up, she left the boy under one of the bushes. Then she went and sat down opposite him, about a bowshot away, for she said, "Do not let me see the boy die." And she sat opposite him and lifted up her voice and wept. God heard the lad crying; and the angel of God called to Hagar from heaven and said to her, "What is the matter with you, Hagar? Do not fear, for God has heard the voice of the lad where he is. Arise, lift up the lad, and hold him by the hand, for I will make a great nation of him." Then God opened her eyes and she saw a well of water; and she went and filled the skin with water and gave the lad a drink.*
> *(Genesis 21:14-19)*

God opened the eyes of Hagar to see what she had not seen before: a well of water. For what appeared to be the end of the road from a distraught woman's viewpoint was actually a new beginning from God's viewpoint. Hagar had sat down, as if to put a period on the end of her life. Yet God was calling her to get up.

In verse 18 God stated, "Arise, lift up the lad, and hold him by the hand, for I will make a great nation of him." God was calling Hagar to arise, take hold of her child, and move forward according to the promise He had given to her. You see, the chapter in which Hagar found herself was not the last page of her story. Instead, aligned with a new beginning, a new chapter emerged. For in Hagar's life, yellow flowers were blooming even though her eyes were not open to see them at the time.

What scene in your life is currently holding your attention? Are you standing in a messy and sluggish place? Are you in a desert of desolation and hopelessness? Arise, look up, and take God by the hand. For He is not finished with you, and He is not finished with your future. Ask the Lord to open your eyes to see what you may not currently be seeing. Ask Him to let you see those yellow flowers of blessings.

Lord, please help me . . .

____

____

____

____

____

____

____

Standing on the Other Side of Our Dreams

Delight yourself in the LORD;
And He will give you the desires of your heart.
—Psalm 37:4

I was invited to speak to employees at twelve different restaurants in the Dallas/Fort Worth (DFW) area in Texas. This was a dream come true, as I had desired for years to engage in biblically based motivational speaking. As I arrived at the first restaurant, I walked inside in anticipation of the time they would give me to bring forth a message God had planted in my heart—a message I was excited to share.

As I walked into the main entrance, Mr. Paul, the owner, met me. We spoke briefly about the upcoming talk. Afterwards, Mr. Paul ventured toward the kitchen where he stood for a time, watching individuals prepare for the upcoming lunch hour. As I observed him from a distance, standing in a kitchen he had once dreamed of building, the thought instantly came to my mind that Mr. Paul was now standing on the other side of his dream. What had started out as a vision was now a reality. What had started out as one restaurant had now turned into fourteen restaurants. Today, Babes Chicken stands as one of the most popular restaurants in the DFW area. The owner was now enjoying the fruits of not only his labor but a dream planted within his heart many years prior.

On that same day, I, too, was standing on the other side of my dream. Years prior, I had desired to engage in motivational speaking, but doors never seemed to open as I hoped. For a time, I pushed it aside, yet I still desired to see it happen. Finally, and in God's timing, I was now beginning to see the desire come to fruition.

> *Trust in the LORD and do good;*
> *Dwell in the land and cultivate faithfulness.*
> *Delight yourself in the LORD;*
> *And He will give you the desires of your heart.*
> *Commit your way to the LORD,*
> *Trust also in Him, and He will do it.*
> *He will bring forth your righteousness as the light*
> *And your judgment as the noonday.*
> *(Psalm 37:3-6)*

God tells us that when we delight ourselves in Him, He will give us the desires of our hearts. God places His desires within our hearts and then brings those desires to fruition at the appointed time. During those seasons of waiting, He is working—not only within our hearts but through us in preparation for the desired dream. He is moving in other people's hearts, readying them to be a part of the dream. He is shifting, pruning, and setting everything in motion for the very day when those dreams become reality.

Because we may not see anything happening at the moment does not mean God is not working. He is always working and moving us toward His perfect will for our lives. His perfect will includes the desires He has placed within our hearts.

One of the prayers I often pray is for God to remove any desire from my heart that is not of Him. Why? Because the more I come to know

Him and trust Him, the more I come to understand God knows what is best for my life. *Period.* My desire may be for something not of Him, and when He shows me that truth, I can trust that His will for my life is best.

Where do you find yourself at today in your dream? Are you at the beginning stages? Is something currently stirring in your heart? Are you sensing God's leading in any direction? Do you have a passion to serve in a particular area in your church or in your community? Pay attention to the desires of your heart, and then bring them before God to seek His direction. If He plants the desires, He will bring them to fruition in His appointed time. Just like Mr. Paul and countless others who have gone before us, we, too, will one day be standing on the other side of the dream, enjoying the fruits of our labors.

Lord, please help me . . .

____

____

____

____

____

____

____

A Heart That Is Wounded Cries Loudly Through Actions

Watch over your heart with all diligence,
For from it flow the springs of life.
—Proverbs 4:23

He was a dear brother. His nickname: *Mustard Seed.* He walked with God in a way that Sadie most admired, and he heard from the Lord in a manner she deeply desired for herself. Sadie greatly respected her brother's love for Jesus, his love for his wife, and his love for others. Yet one thing with which she struggled was her brother's readiness to confront issues within *her* life, even though he did so in grace and love.

One day, Sadie was met by her brother's assertion that arrested her attention to a matter she had tried hard to avoid. The topic? An unhealed heart. Her brother had recognized a bruised soul in his sister that was producing unwarranted behavior. Yet instead of listening to wise counsel, Sadie immediately refuted such claims. Her actions reflected her true heart's condition way more than any words she offered in defense to her brother's discovery.

> *As in water face reflects face,*
> *So the heart of man reflects man.*
> *(Proverbs 27:19)*

No matter the mask we attempt to put on or the outward apparel we drape around us, God sees our hearts. Before her brother had ever spoken to Sadie about her fractured heart, the Holy Spirit had already revealed the issue.

God sees our hearts.

> *"For God sees not as man sees, for man looks at the*
> *outward appearance, but the LORD looks at the heart."*
> *(1 Samuel 16:7)*

God is the healer of our souls.

> *He heals the brokenhearted*
> *And binds up their wounds.*
> *(Psalm 147:3)*

God knows when our hearts are bleeding inside from our wounds. He sees the sections of our souls that are sourced as burial sites, holding undealt issues long submerged. Yet God desires to resurrect those hurts in order to place His balm of Gilead, Jesus Himself, on the root of the cause.

When the Holy Spirit reveals areas in your heart needing attention, listen to Him and be obedient to what He is asking you to do. What you may be ignoring repeatedly may be the one thing hindering God's work in your life. Do not let pride stop you from bending a knee to your healing. God is only a call away. Let Him in, let Him work, and let Him heal.

Instead of deeming those *Mustard Seeds* (Christian brothers or sisters) as bothersome, view them as instruments in God's hands. For the

Lord may use each one to reveal things to which our pride has long blinded us.

Lord, please help me . . .

____

____

____

____

____

____

____

____

____

Lord, please help me . . .

For Such a Time as This, You Have Been Placed and Positioned

"For if you remain silent at this time, relief and deliverance will arise for the Jews from another place and you and your father's house will perish. And who knows whether you have not attained royalty for such a time as this?"
—Esther 4:14

At a young age, Esther had been orphaned and taken in to be raised by her uncle, Mordecai. However, years later, she found herself in a royal position. Esther had been placed, positioned, and chosen to be queen to King Ahasuerus. Mordecai and Esther were both Jews; however, the news of their Jewish descent had not yet been revealed to the king.

Following Esther's royal appointment, Haman emerged with a plot to destroy the Jews. Not only was the individual's plan heard by King Ahasuerus, but the king approved it as well. Unbeknownst to Esther, an edict was sent out ordering the assassination of many Jews. After Mordecai received the news, Esther was summoned to help in a very profound way:

> *When Mordecai learned all that had been done, he tore his clothes, put on sackcloth and ashes, and went out into the midst of the city and wailed loudly and bitterly. He went as far as the king's gate, for no one was to enter the king's gate clothed in sackcloth. In each and every province where the command and decree of the king came, there was great mourning among the Jews, with fasting, weeping and wailing; and many lay on sackcloth and ashes. Then Esther's maidens and her eunuchs came and told her, and the queen writhed in great anguish. And she sent garments to clothe Mordecai that he might remove his sackcloth from him, but he did not accept them. Then Esther summoned Hathach from the king's eunuchs, whom the king had appointed to attend her, and ordered him to go to Mordecai to learn what this was and why it was. So Hathach went out to Mordecai to the city square in front of the king's gate. Mordecai told him all that had happened to him, and the exact amount of money that Haman had promised to pay to the king's treasuries for the destruction of the Jews. He also gave him a copy of the text of the edict which had been issued in Susa for their destruction, that he might show Esther and inform her, and to order her to go in to the king to implore his favor and to plead with him for her people. Hathach came back and related Mordecai's words to Esther.*
> *(Esther 4:1-9)*

After Queen Esther learned of the conspiracy against the Jews and of Mordecai's request, she felt powerless to comply with her uncle's appeal. For in order to see the king, one had to be summoned by him, or one would face death—unless the king held out his golden scepter. Queen Esther attempted to explain to her uncle that the King had not summoned her for many days.

> ***Then Esther spoke to Hathach and ordered him to reply to Mordecai: "All the king's servants and the people of the king's provinces know that for any man or woman who comes to the king to the inner court who is not summoned, he has but one law, that he be put to death, unless the king holds out to him the golden scepter so that he may live. And I have not been summoned to come to the king for these thirty days." They related Esther's words to Mordecai.***
> ***(Esther 4:10-12)***

As Queen Esther's message was relayed to Mordecai, he then responded with a message of his own.

> ***Then Mordecai told them to reply to Esther, "Do not imagine that you in the king's palace can escape any more than all the Jews. For if you remain silent at this time, relief and deliverance will arise for the Jews from another place and you and your father's house will perish. And who knows whether you have not attained royalty for such a time as this?"***
> ***(Esther 4:13-14)***

Never doubt that where you have been placed and positioned has a much bigger plan and purpose than what you may realize. Esther soon understood that the crown that she wore would denote more than just a glamorous position; rather, it would be tied to a call to courage and a call of action.

For such a time as this, we have been placed where we are to help build God's kingdom and to carry out those special assignments He has ordained for our lives. For such a time as this, we have been called to rear up our children in God's truth and direction. For such a time as this, we have been called to share the gospel message with a broken and hurting world. And for such a time as this, Queen Esther was called to risk it all—to stand for her people.

After receiving Mordecai's message, Queen Esther realized what she had to do. Further, she came to understand why she had been placed in such a royal position. To say the least, her response to her uncle was both courageous and inspiring.

> *Then Esther told them to reply to Mordecai, "Go, assemble all the Jews who are found in Susa, and fast for me; do not eat or drink for three days, night or day. I and my maidens also will fast in the same way. And thus I will go in to the king, which is not according to the law; and if I perish, I perish." So Mordecai went away and did just as Esther had commanded him.*
> *(Esther 4:15-17)*

Queen Esther realized what was at stake, yet she was willing and ready to act on behalf of her people—even if it meant losing her own life. Her bold decision to be courageous and act kept the Jews from being destroyed, which included the life of her uncle, Mordecai, as well as her own.

See your placement and position as an assignment from the Lord, with the promise that He will never leave you nor forsake you. Onward, mighty women and men of God; the Lord is up to something where He has positioned you. Trust Him! Open up your ears to listen and your eyes to see, for you never know when the day will come when you, too, will be called *for such a time as this* to be used greatly for God's kingdom. Be ready!

Lord, please help me . . .

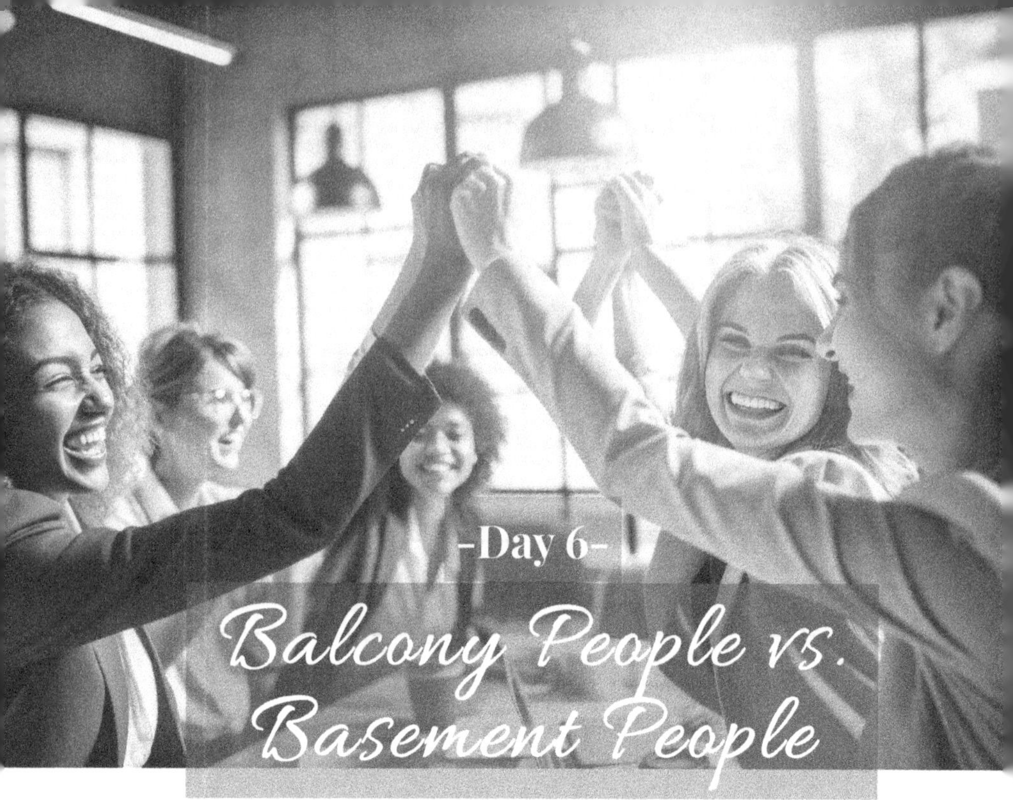

Therefore encourage one another and build up one another, just as you also are doing.
—1 Thessalonians 5:11

I had the wonderful privilege of attending Blue Mountain Christian University (BMCU) in my early twenties, preparing educationally for a life of ministry. Chapel attendance was important at BMCU, and the lessons that transpired from attendance were highly regarded. One such discourse I recall came from a woman who presented on two manners of people: *balcony people* vs. *basement people*. To this day, I remember not only the magnitude of the lady's message but the life-changing implications her conversation awarded.

Balcony people are best described as encouraging individuals while *basement people* are pessimistic. I have entertained both types of persons in my life, resulting in both positive and negative influences. Nevertheless, the lessons I have learned remain transformative to this day.

Balcony People

Throughout my life, there have been countless doors open to engage in both ministry- and job-related opportunities. I remember a number of persons who would stand on their balconies, leaning over to cheer faithfully as I ran my race relentlessly. Not only immediate family members but church family members, pastors, friends, and professors have all contributed to my pursuits as great encouragers.

The lessons I've learned and blessings I've obtained as a result of having these balcony people in my life are too numerous to count. Through their examples, I have learned how to encourage others in a positive way. Through their influence, I have been encouraged as well as motivated to go the extra mile while giving my best to the race set before me.

A positive impact of balcony people is that I realize the significance of being affirmative and supportive of individuals in my life. I have also been inspired to cheer others on in their journeys, just as I have witnessed in my own life.

Basement People

I believe everyone, at some point or another, has experienced a situation where an individual in their life has delivered discouragement to dreams and special callings. The Bible provides such a strong example with the Pharisees who doubted, debated, and even discouraged others. I, too, have experienced the disrespect from Pharisees in my own life. Though time will not permit me to list such affronts, time does allow me to share lessons learned from such persons.

Through basement people, I saw a picture of destructiveness, helping me strive to move away from such conduct. There is no solution in pessimism, only a lack of belief. Through their influence, I have learned not to allow people's unbelief to impact my walk, guide my path, or even shape my thinking. I realized early on in my life that God can open doors—or He can close them—in spite of what others might believe. The skepticism people have has no authority to stop what God has divinely called.

As a positive result of basement people, I have come to learn how imperative it is to love and pray for those who hold to a form of negativity in their lives toward others. I have furthermore discovered that even though such individuals may exist in our lives, we should never give power to them.

In the book of Nehemiah, we see an example of a great man of God who has been called to rebuild the ruins of his hometown. It was a huge yet risky task, to say the least; however, Nehemiah committed to the task at hand. As soon as he began God's work, trouble persisted. Not once but several times individuals attempted to derail the work of this man of God. They doubted, discouraged, and even disheartened the people who were assisting the labor. At one point, these persons, whom I will call "basement people," ordered Nehemiah to come down from his work. Yet the man of God refused to give in to their bluff.

> *Now when it was reported to Sanballat, Tobiah, to Geshem the Arab and to the rest of our enemies that I had rebuilt the wall, and that no breach remained in it, although at that time I had not set up the doors in the gates, then Sanballat and Geshem sent a message to me, saying, "Come, let us meet together at Chephirim in the plain of Ono." But they were planning to harm me. So I sent messengers to them, saying, "I am doing a great work and I cannot come down. Why should the work stop while I leave it and come down to you?"*
> *(Nehemiah 6:1-3)*

The same question could be conveyed today in regard to man's attempts to discourage our race: *Why should the work stop while I leave it and come down to you?* We must keep moving forward with God, no matter what.

Do you have someone in your church whom God is using greatly? Cheer him or her on! Do you have an individual pursing a call from God? Lean way over your balcony and shout loudly, "I am praying for you." Encouragement always breeds hope, while discouragement generates hopelessness. Choose today to encourage others to live their lives fully in Christ.

One final thought and a word of caution: Be careful not to seek the approval or even the cheers of others. Even though having balcony people in one's life is important, it is God's cheers that trump man's applause. He is the biggest and most important balcony Person of all, and at the end of the day, it is His words that matter most.

Lord, please help me . . .

____

____

____

____

____

____

____

Brethren, I do not regard myself as having laid hold of it yet; but one thing I do: forgetting what lies behind and reaching forward to what lies ahead, I press on toward the goal for the prize of the upward call of God in Christ Jesus.
—Philippians 3:13-14

Countless people today are nurturing their pasts with great care. Instead of bringing their history to Christ, they have continued to advance with broken hearts over past failures they have never fully dealt with. As a result, many remain captives of their former days, allowing the feeling of shame to rule in their lives instead of the peace of God.

Therefore there is now no condemnation for those who are in Christ Jesus.
(Romans 8:1)

I spent numerous years running from my *yesterdays*, and I suffered greatly for it. I felt it was too painful to discuss my past with God.

I was embarrassed by the choices I had made, and I feared anyone finding out. Yet my denial to face my Savior was delaying the healing He so desired to bring.

I remember frequent periods where the enemy would tempt me to dwell on the uncertainties of my future due to past mistakes. Yet I eventually came to realize the enemy was devising a strategic plan to build strongholds. Satan knew if he could keep me living in fear, I would never embrace or even know the freedom God so longed to give me. This fear is a tool of the enemy to keep us in bondage to our pasts, and when we surrender to its power, it will have a crippling impact on our lives. But in Isaiah 41:10, God tells us not to fear for the sole reason that He is with us.

I know firsthand how painful and scary it is to bring our pasts to Christ, but I also know the freedom that comes from doing so. I had to entrust not only my past to God but my disappointments and shame as well.

Casting all your anxiety on Him, because He cares
for you.
(1 Peter 5:7)

One evening, I walked into my closet, sat down in the dark, and through the Spirit's guidance, made a decision to bring my history to God. In that moment, His grace collided with my shame, overtaking my broken heart with love. God gave me the courage to bring my past to His throne room of grace, and grace was just what I experienced. No more bandages placed upon my life's issues, but instead, a divine intervention by God Himself. He wanted my yesterdays so He could give me His tomorrows of new beginnings. He wanted my fears so He could grant me His peace.

For God has not given us a spirit of timidity, but of
power and love and discipline.
(2 Timothy 1:7)

God says in His Word that when we repent of our sins, He is faithful to forgive those sins and remember them no more. After confession and repentance, the enemy tried hard to pull out the files from my past and force me to review them in my mind. Yet I learned a valuable truth: whatever we allow to draw our attention will certainly captivate our hearts. Let me voice this once again: *whatever we allow to draw our attention (past mistakes that we choose to linger on—or—God's truth) will certainly captivate our hearts.* When we linger on the past, we will stay in bondage; however, when we focus on God's truth, we will walk in freedom.

When I relinquished everything to God—my past and all my mistakes—He began a most amazing work in my heart. One that I stand amazed by to this day.

> **God is our refuge and strength,**
> **A very present help in trouble.**
> **(Psalm 46:1)**

We can't change our past, but what we can do is place it in God's hands. Choose today to bring your past to Christ, knowing with certainty that you are safe in His hands in doing so. He is our Redeemer and Restorer, making all things new! Let God hold you, not your past. Let God define you, not your past. Take courage, and bring it all to Him.

Lord, please help me . . .

Let us not lose heart in doing good, for in due time we will reap if
we do not grow weary.
—Galatians 6:9

A beautiful Thursday morning dawned as the ship set out on a journey toward a desired destination. The waters were calm and the sky blue as the vessel drifted away from the harbor. Yet, many hours into the voyage, the ship encountered a fierce storm, rapidly turning the once-secure journey into a perilous one.

By nightfall, intensifying winds strengthened the storm. Beaten and battered by the waves, the vessel began to lose control. The sky was now black, and the fog was so thick one could barely see what lay ahead. As the hours drifted slowly by and the ship was caught up and driven by the wind, the precarious scene began to depict hopelessness. By this time, the captain had abandoned all hope. What he didn't know, however, was that what appeared to be the end of a journey was about to be met by divine intervention.

Way into the night, the captain of the ship spotted a bright light piercing the fog. The light was the beam from a lighthouse that stood beautifully on a nearby shore. The only thing the captain could see was the ray of light as he fought fiercely to gain control of the wheel. After securing control, he steered the ship toward the beam until he reached the safety of the shore.

Due to the overwhelming presence of the storm, the captain could not see the shoreline to lead the ship to a safe harbor. For a period, the captain listened more to the tempest cries than to any whispers of hope. We, too, have been on that same ship at one time or another in our lives—a ship tossed and turned by the waves of a troubling storm, a scene depicting hopelessness rather than victory. For a moment recently, I was in that ship. I was on a journey in which I felt secure, and I thought I was heading in a certain direction. All of a sudden, my path took an unanticipated turn, and before I knew it, I was caught up in the strength of that storm.

After days of being tossed by the effects of the tempest, I stepped into my closet, sat down on the floor, and cried out to God. Questions began to flow to the Lord, as confusion was attempting to trample out my faith. Had I heard wrongly from God? Suddenly a ray of a light beaming through a very thick fog of uncertainty illuminated my heart, revealing a particular passage of scripture. The light was none other than God's personal Word for my situation:

> *Let us hold fast the confession of our hope without wavering, for He who promised is faithful.*
> *(Hebrews 10:23)*

> *And without faith it is impossible to please Him, for he who comes to God must believe that He is and that He is a rewarder of those who seek Him.*
> *(Hebrews 11:6)*

On this day, I was reminded that God is faithful to His promises *and* to His child. No storm or thick fog can prevent His promises from being brought to fruition. God's Word was the piercing ray of hope that led me safely to a harbor of renewed faith and unshakeable hope.

> ***Therefore, my beloved brethren, be steadfast, immovable, always abounding in the work of the Lord, knowing that your toil is not in vain in the Lord.***
> ***(1 Corinthians 15:58)***

Remember, just because circumstances may appear hopeless does not mean they are hopeless. Suddenly, He will come. Suddenly, His light will pierce through your darkness. Suddenly, your once out-of-control ship will regain control and veer toward a safe harbor of faithfulness instead of faithlessness. Hold on to God's promises; your *suddenly* is coming.

Lord, please help me . . .

____

____

____

____

____

____

____

Yet those who wait for the LORD
Will gain new strength;
They will mount up with wings like eagles,
They will run and not get tired,
They will walk and not become weary.
—Isaiah 40:31

A recent insert from my prayer journal reminded me once again of God's great faithfulness to His word and to His children. At one point in my life, an unexpected opportunity was presented to me that seemed both interesting and sensible to pursue. However, as I went before the Lord to seek His will on the matter, He immediately led me to a passage in the book of Joshua, one where the Israelites were called to wait until God moved:

Then Joshua rose early in the morning; and he and
all the sons of Israel set out from Shittim and came to
the Jordan, and they lodged there before they crossed.

> *At the end of three days the officers went through the midst of the camp; and they commanded the people, saying, "When you see the ark of the covenant of the Lord your God with the Levitical priests carrying it, then you shall set out from your place and go after it."*
> *(Joshua 3:1-3)*

The children of Israel were standing at the Jordan, awaiting their time to cross in order to enter the Promised Land. Joshua's command was clear: when they saw the ark of the covenant, they were to move forward. But until that moment arrived, they were to remain in the camp. In other words, they were not to proceed forward until God moved first.

On the day I read this passage of scripture, I knew God was telling me to wait. I was not to pursue what seemed logical or even appealing. God knew that on the other side of His call to wait was a greater blessing than what I had anticipated. While I only saw the opportunity, God saw the bigger picture—one that included a plan He was getting ready to unfold and one that did not include the opening I had longed to pursue.

I love the game of football. One scene has always captured my attention due to the spiritual lesson it portrays: the locale of the coaches. During both college and NFL games, the head coaches—as well as various assistants—will be located on the sidelines. For the most part, however, both the defensive coaches as well as the offensive coordinators will position themselves in the press box. Why? The answer is simple. While the coaches on the sidelines merely perceive a limited view, the coaches in the press box see the entirety of the game. Many deem the press box as the "eyes in the sky."

As Christians, we too have "eyes in the sky." We have a Savior who sees the totality of our lives, from beginning to end. Therefore, when He says wait, we can rest in knowing that He sees beyond what is in front of us to what He has in store for us. Remember: when you and I are tempted to plunge ahead, according to what we think is best, we may miss God's best.

Trust in the Lord with all your heart
And do not lean on your own understanding.
In all your ways acknowledge Him,
And He will make your paths straight.
(Proverbs 3:5-6)

When we become anxious in the waiting, remember: God is weaving things together for His glory and for our good, and that includes waiting times.

Therefore the Lord longs to be gracious to you,
And therefore He waits on high to have compassion
on you.
For the Lord is a God of justice;
How blessed are all those who long for Him.
(Isaiah 30:18)

Are you struggling with your sideline view? Are you seeking God for direction? Keep praying, and know with confidence that God hears you and will act in His perfect timing. For just around the corner, your miracle awaits. God will usher in your blessing at just the right time. However, until that moment arrives—and it will—remember to wait. And in the waiting, trust Him.

I would have despaired unless I had believed that I
would see the goodness of the Lord
In the land of the living.
Wait for the Lord;
Be strong and let your heart take courage;
Yes, wait for the Lord.
(Psalm 27:13-14)

Lord, please help me . . .

____

____

____

____

____

____

____

____

____

____

It came about at the seventh time, that he said, "Behold, a cloud as small as a man's hand is coming up from the sea." And he said, "Go up, say to Ahab, 'Prepare your chariot and go down, so that the heavy shower does not stop you.'"
—1 Kings 18:44

In the deep crevices of my heart, I had attempted to bury a request that I had longed for God to answer. I had concluded in my own reasoning that it was a hopeless situation. However, later, to my surprise, I discovered that even though I had resigned all hope of the request being answered, God was not finished with the matter.

One day while attending church, I felt a tremendous compulsion to pray over the situation. When I arrived home, I went before God with the request. With all my heart and with great confidence, I felt the liberty to petition Him to act on my behalf in the matter. What I had attempted to bury, God resurrected with an intense call to beseech Him. He wanted me to be honest about what was in my heart. Shortly after a long period of prayer, I came to 1 Kings 18, where Elijah had prayed for rain. As I continued to read the passage, three words gripped my heart: *prepare your chariot.*

> *Now Elijah said to Ahab, "Go up, eat and drink; for there is the sound of the roar of a heavy shower." So Ahab went up to eat and drink. But Elijah went up to the top of Carmel; and he crouched down on the earth and put his face between his knees. He said to his servant, "Go up now, look toward the sea." So he went up and looked and said, "There is nothing." And he said, "Go back" seven times. It came about at the seventh time, that he said, "Behold, a cloud as small as a man's hand is coming up from the sea." And he said, "Go up, say to Ahab, 'Prepare your chariot and go down, so that the heavy shower does not stop you.'" In a little while the sky grew black with clouds and wind, and there was a heavy shower. And Ahab rode and went to Jezreel. Then the hand of the Lord was on Elijah, and he girded up his loins and outran Ahab to Jezreel.*
> *(1 Kings 18:41-46)*

What truths can we glean from this passage? First, *Elijah took his petition before the Lord.* Only God could answer such a request—and He would, for He had earlier promised Elijah rain. Elijah trusted God and knew He would be faithful to His word. Second, *Elijah refused to allow the scene in front of him to speak louder than God's word to him.* The scene depicted no sight of rain, yet this did not deter Elijah from seeking God. After a time of prayer, Elijah made the following request of his servant: "Go up now, look toward the sea." In other words, Elijah was asking, "Do you see anything that looks like rain approaching?" The servant did as Elijah requested. He turned to see if there was any sign of rain. He then replied to Elijah, "There is nothing."

Third, *Elijah refused to give up believing.* He continued to push through in prayer with a resolve to believe that God would come through. When his servant stated, "There is nothing," Elijah did not say, "Oh well, I guess I missed it." Instead, he commanded his servant to "go back" seven times. The servant did as Elijah requested; he went back seven times. Afterward, he returned to Elijah to share that a small cloud was evolving. Then, Elijah responded, "Go up, say to Ahab, 'Prepare your chariot and go down, so that the heavy shower does not stop you'" (v. 44). Elijah gave orders to "prepare your chariot" before one drop of rain had fallen. He knew the rain was on its way. God had earlier told Elijah that He would send rain. Elijah took God at His word, prayed, and believed the miracle of rain would come—even when it appeared hopeless.

We can bring daily our petitions to God, for only He can intervene in our situation. Yet as we wait on God to act, we must guard against allowing the scene in front of us to dictate our faith. Even though we may not see anything happening, that doesn't mean it isn't. We must trust that God is at work (Romans 8:28-29; 2 Corinthians 5:7). We must be willing to push through those hard times, refusing to give up in prayer, until God answers (James 5:16). And lastly, we must trust God as we wait on Him to act on our behalf according to His perfect will (Proverbs 3:5-7).

One never knows what God is getting ready to do, so don't stop praying. Remember, while you and I only see what is in front of us, God sees the bigger picture. What are you needing God to do on your behalf? What have you buried in the crevices of your heart? What have you given up on? Go back, start praying, go back, keep believing, go back, and listen to the voice of God. Then, "Prepare your chariot."

Lord, please help me . . .

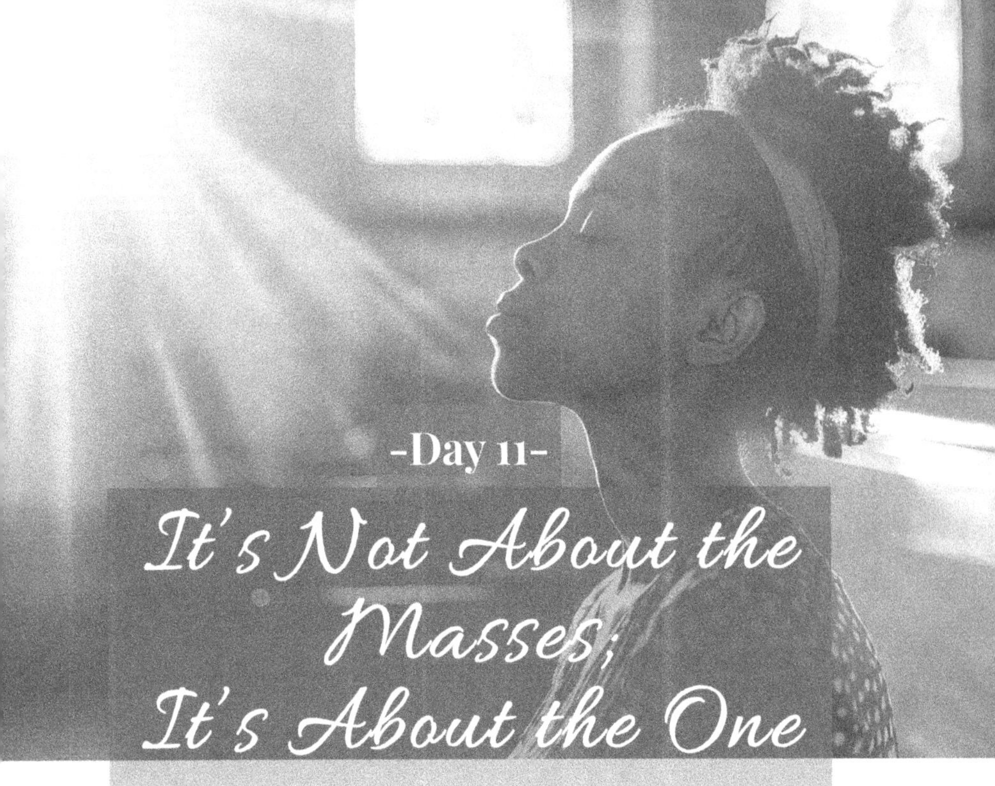

It's Not About the Masses; It's About the One

One of the two who heard John speak and followed Him, was Andrew, Simon Peter's brother. He found first his own brother Simon and said to him, "We have found the Messiah" (which translated means Christ). He brought him to Jesus. Jesus looked at him and said, "You are Simon the son of John; you shall be called Cephas" (which is translated Peter).
—John 1:40-42

Years ago, the Lord called a woman into full-time Christian ministry. He placed her in a particular setting wherein He wanted her to minister. Developing projects for the local church was her passion, as was writing, which she enjoyed immensely.

One day, this woman's focus began to shift. She began to doubt if what she was doing was even making a difference. She had worked tirelessly on countless assignments, while seemingly impacting only a few. Finally, this disheartened woman went before the Lord in prayer. She reminded God on this day that He had called many individuals to ministry and was using them to influence a myriad of people. With a scarce few she seemed to be reaching, she wondered if the continued effort was worth it. She even began to doubt her usefulness to the Lord. Out of desperation, the woman posed a question to God: *What can I bring to the table?* Discouragement clouded her call as well as the Lord's overall mission for her life.

As the woman continued spending time with the Lord, a long-ago story came to her mind. The story reminded her of God's love—not only for the *masses* but also for *the one*.

The story began with a troubled woman walking along the shoreline of the beach. She saw at a distance a man throwing things into the ocean. The closer they got to each other, she realized he was throwing starfish back into the water. She asked him why he was doing that, and he said because he didn't want them to get scorched by the sun and die. She said that there were countless starfish along miles of coastline; why would this make any difference at all? To this he responded, "It makes a difference for this one."[1]

After reading this story, the woman knew God was ministering to her heart, reminding her she was making a difference—one person at a time. Afterwards, the woman picked up her computer to check her emails. To her surprise, she had received a message that would echo what God was attempting to teach her on this day. The email stated,

> *Thank you for writing to encourage so many that needed to hear this, including me.*

As she pondered over the email, this woman became fixated on the words *including me.* On this day, she became encouraged by a powerful message God was teaching her. It is not about the masses but about the one. For when you reach the *one*, that *one* will reach another *one*, and these *ones* will become the *masses*.

---

1. Based on "The Star Thrower" from *The Unexpected Universe* by Loren Eiseley. Copyright © 1968 by Loren Eiseley and renewed 1996 by John A. Eichman, III.

In John 1, we read a powerful story of how Jesus reached the people, one person at a time.

> *Again the next day John was standing with two of his disciples, and he looked at Jesus as He walked, and said, "Behold, the Lamb of God!" The two disciples heard him speak, and they followed Jesus. And Jesus turned and saw them following, and said to them, "What do you seek?" They said to Him, "Rabbi (which translated means Teacher), where are You staying?" He said to them, "Come, and you will see." So they came and saw where He was staying; and they stayed with Him that day, for it was about the tenth hour. One of the two who heard John speak and followed Him, was Andrew, Simon Peter's brother. He found first his own brother Simon and said to him, "We have found the Messiah" (which translated means Christ). He brought him to Jesus. Jesus looked at him and said, "You are Simon the son of John; you shall be called Cephas" (which is translated Peter).*
> *(John 1:35-42)*

Notice in verse 41: "He found first his own brother Simon." Simon was one person, but look how God used him to reach the masses:

> *The next day He purposed to go into Galilee, and He found Philip. And Jesus said to him, "Follow Me." Now Philip was from Bethsaida, of the city of Andrew and Peter. Philip found Nathanael and said to him, "We have found Him of whom Moses in the Law and also the Prophets wrote—Jesus*

> *of Nazareth, the son of Joseph."*
> *(John 1:43-45)*

Notice: "Philip found Nathanael."

> *Jesus saw Nathanael coming to Him, and said*
> *of him, "Behold, an Israelite indeed, in whom*
> *there is no deceit!" Nathanael said to Him, "How*
> *do You know me?" Jesus answered and said to*
> *him, "Before Philip called you, when you were under*
> *the fig tree, I saw you."*
> *(John 1:47-48)*

Notice: Jesus saw *the one*!

God cares as much for the *one* as He does for the *masses*. Let us set our minds on following Jesus—finding those Simons, those Philips, those Nathanaels—one person at a time. See to the one to whom God has entrusted you to minister.

Lord, please help me . . .

Now to Him who is able to do far more abundantly beyond all that we ask or think, according to the power that works within us, to Him be the glory in the church and in Christ Jesus to all generations forever and ever. Amen.
—Ephesians 3:20-21

The big day had finally arrived. After numerous years in college and seminary, the date was set for me to give my defense for my doctoral studies—the culmination of my seminary degree. As I walked into the room where I would be meeting with my professors, I took my seat on the right side of a long, large table. As I sat quietly awaiting the arrival of my professors, I began to reminisce on a prior semester in which one of my classes was held in that very classroom. During that particular semester, I always took my seat on the left side of the table; on this day, however, I was seated on the opposite side.

As I looked over at the seat I had once occupied, a thought came to my mind in the form of a question: *When you were sitting over there, did you ever think you would be sitting here?* As I reflected on this thought, I was immediately overwhelmed with thanksgiving to the Lord for His faithfulness in where He had brought me, all for His glory and His kingdom work. However, this basking was quickly disrupted when my focus was redirected to a wooden chair in the corner of the room. This chair, which appeared restricted, reminded me of those seasons of my life when people tried hard to *pick the seats* they desired me to occupy in order to restrict my usefulness and my movement toward the great things God had waiting for me. Numerous chairs sat in sundry corners. But then . . . Jesus.

In case someone today finds themselves in a similar situation, I wish to share a particular memory in order to convey a few lessons I learned. I recall a time in my early thirties when I walked into a restaurant, and a man was seated at a table with two other gentlemen. As I turned the corner to take my seat at another table, the man went to great lengths to make sure I heard his loud, boisterous remark, alluding to the type of student I had once been. To say the least, his comment was unkind. As laughter roared from the three men at that table, I continued moving toward my table where I pulled out a chair and sat down in utter humiliation. Little did I know then that years later I would find myself sitting at yet another table, where God Himself had pulled out a chair for me to sit down in. The gentleman only recounted who I used to be; however, the Lord saw what I would become through Him.

Lessons Learned

Due to unbelief and jealousies, some individuals in our lives may attempt to "seat us" in particular chairs in which they feel we belong. When this happens, remember the following truths: (1) God will use those moments to grow us and to make us more like Jesus. He will use those periods to teach us invaluable lessons. We must be good students, not pouty ones. Learn well. (2) We must let such moments encourage rather than derail us. We may have our feelings hurt, but don't let the enemy have the victory. Do not grow bitter toward others. Pray, forgive, and love. Allow God's truth to lead you, and keep moving. (3) Let God seat you—not man. Never give power to people to determine your future. It is God's will that will prevail, not the will of man. Others' unbelief in us will never stop God's will for us. Onward! Embrace your calling. Allow God to pull out the chair He desires for you to occupy.

Where you find yourself sitting today may not be where you find yourself sitting tomorrow. Allow God to have His perfect will and way in your life so that you will reach the destiny that He has ordained for you. For God wants to do more in your life than you could ever dream or imagine.

I will always be thankful for the day I sat at that table at Southwestern Baptist Theological Seminary and heard those two professors state, "You passed your defense." Yet, to be honest, I am even more grateful for the process I went through to get there, including that day at the restaurant. God pulled out His chair for me and showered me with His blessings, not shame. Remember, God uses everything for His glory and His kingdom building, even a small-town, country girl who never envisioned herself as a doctoral student and who, at one time, thought the sidelines of life was where she belonged.

B.U.T. T.H.E.N. J.E.S.U.S.

Let God seat you.

Lord, please help me . . .

A Desolate Situation Met by a Savior

And He said, "Bring them here to Me."
—Matthew 14:18

S he had found herself in a desolate place. From a deep pit, she cried out many times but felt as though no one heard her. She tried every way possible to escape the trial that was wreaking havoc on her life instead of allowing her Savior to teach and mold her through it. She devised numerous strategies, based on her own understanding, to better deal with her situation. Yet one by one, her plans crumbled. Finally, she gave up. She no longer believed that she could obtain help in the middle of her desolate situation. But what appeared to be impossible was soon to be met by a miracle worker—a Savior, who would not only step on the scene of her situation but would turn it all around for His glory and for her good. The woman's hopelessness was met by God's faithfulness.

Throughout God's Word, we read of countless moments when hopelessness was met by miracles.

> *Now when Jesus heard about John, He withdrew from there in a boat to a secluded place by Himself; and when the people heard of this, they followed Him on foot from the cities. When He went ashore, He saw a large crowd, and felt compassion for them and healed their sick.*
> *(Matthew 14:13-14)*

Jesus was stirred with compassion for the people He encountered. He realized they were like "sheep without a Shepherd." He spent time instructing the people as well as healing the sick. It was important to Jesus then (as it is today) to minister to His creation.

> *As the day began to draw to a close, the disciples approached Jesus with a declaration, as well as a plan for an urgent need they observed: When it was evening, the disciples came to Him and said, "This place is desolate and the hour is already late; so send the crowds away, that they may go into the villages and buy food for themselves." But Jesus said to them, "They do not need to go away; you give them something to eat!" They said to Him, "We have here only five loaves and two fish." And He said, "Bring them here to Me." Ordering the people to sit down on the grass, He took the five loaves and the two fish, and looking up toward heaven, He blessed the food, and breaking the loaves He gave them to the disciples, and the disciples gave them to the crowds, and they all ate and were satisfied. They picked up what was left over of the broken pieces, twelve full baskets. There were about five thousand men who ate, besides women and children.*
> *(Matthew 14:15-21)*

"This place is desolate": This is the first thing the disciples noticed, even declared. In their limited view, the disciples saw the surroundings as a hopeless situation. How in the world could they obtain food from such a place? Before Jesus was given a chance to intervene, the disciples had already determined in their minds that it was *hopeless*. It was desolate.

"The hour is already late": This is the second point the disciples made. How in the world could food (a miracle) be obtained at this hour, especially in a place of desolation? Some of the greatest miracles that Jesus has brought have come at the last hour. God's timing is not our timing. He will come through for you—but in His timing and in His way. Remember, He sees the big picture while you only see the view in front of you. Put your watch down, and let Him work.

"So send the crowds away, that they may go into the villages and buy food for themselves": The disciples' plan of action, for those in need of a miracle, was to send them away. Who did the disciples say this to? Jesus. Who? Jesus. Why would the disciples say to the miracle worker, "Send them away"? Most likely it was because they were leaning on their own understanding of what needed to be done, forgetting that Jesus could bring a miracle anywhere, anytime, even out of a desolate situation.

Jesus listened to the disciple's declaration, then He responded with His own: "They do not need to go away; you give them something to eat!" Jesus knew the miracle that was about to take place. He reminded the disciples of a very important truth: He was the miracle worker. A change of scenery would not bring the miracle, nor would a desolate place stop one from happening.

The disciples replied, "We have here only five loaves and two fish." They seemed to focused more on the scarcity of food than on the Provider Himself.

Jesus stated: "Bring them here to Me." Jesus listened to the disciples' plan of action for feeding the five thousand. He let them talk, share, and describe the dire circumstances. Then, when they had finished, He stepped in, took over, and made a powerful statement: "Bring them here to Me."

On how many occasions do we attempt to fix our own problems? How many instances do we question our Savior's ability to bring forth a miracle? How many times do we debate and even declare the impossibility of a miracle in our desolate situation? Friend, Jesus is still saying today what He said to the disciples back then: "Bring it to Me."

In the hands of a Savior, the loaves and the fish were placed. The result? A miracle. At the beginning of the story, the disciples saw no way to feed the people. Yet after placing the situation in the hands of Jesus, they witnessed the miraculous. Before the miracle, they only saw desolation. After the miracle, they saw Jesus. Yet in all truthfulness, Jesus was there the entire time, even when it looked desolate and hopeless.

The surroundings or circumstances of our situation do not have the final say. Only Jesus does. Desolation does not remove Jesus from the scene; it provides opportunity for a miracle. Instead of telling Jesus how desolate our situation is, let's declare how mighty He will be through it. Let your hopelessness be met by your Savior.

Lord, please help me . . .

____

____

____

____

____

____

____

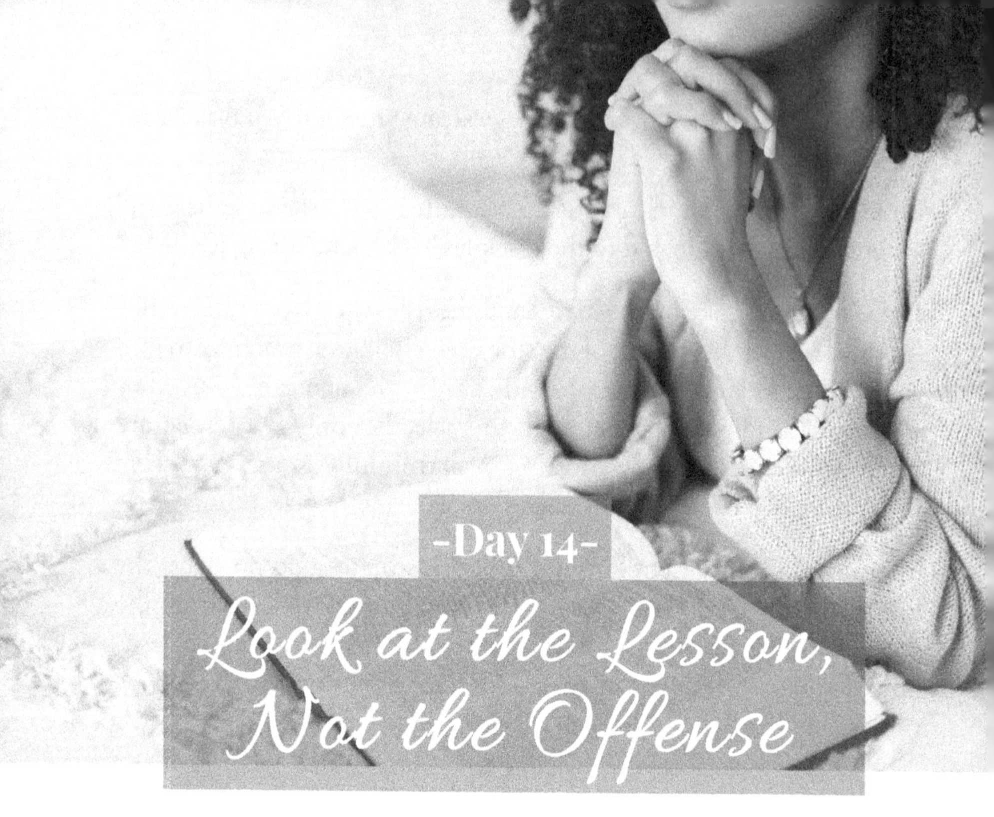

Look at the Lesson, Not the Offense

Love is patient, love is kind and is not jealous; love does not brag and is not arrogant, does not act unbecomingly; it does not seek its own, is not provoked, does not take into account a wrong suffered, does not rejoice in unrighteousness, but rejoices with the truth; bears all things, believes all things, hopes all things, endures all things. Love never fails.
—*1 Corinthians 13:4-8*

One day, as I was carrying out my normal routine, the memory of a past offense abruptly resurfaced. Out of nowhere, the intruder captivated my mind in an attempt to draw my attention to the previous hurt it had once inflicted. As I found myself dwelling on the particular action, my emotions were reaping the consequence of such thinking. However, before it was allowed to linger any longer, the Lord intervened. Suddenly I heard the Holy Spirit whisper to my soul, *Look at the lesson, not the offense.* I knew immediately what the Lord was steering me to remember.

We all have those moments when the Lord teaches us lessons we will never forget. This particular offense birthed such a moment.

The Savior's Classroom vs. The Enemy's Classroom

When an offense comes, you and I will either walk into the classroom where Jesus is the Teacher, or we will walk into the classroom where the enemy presides to instruct. How do we know in which classroom we are? I am glad you asked.

The Savior's Classroom

When we walk into the classroom of our Savior, He will instruct us biblically on how to handle the offense as well as the offender. If we stay with Jesus through it all, diving into His Word and being obedient to what He instructs us to do, we will walk out of that classroom a transformed student—healed, forgiving and loving the person who hurt us, and in awe of the Teacher who instructed us.

The Enemy's Classroom

When an offense comes and we allow ourselves to be instructed by the enemy, we will quickly find ourselves being led toward the following: (1) to view the offense through the eyes of the enemy; (2) to view the person who hurt us through a lens of bitterness; (3) to withhold forgiveness and cling to grudges we were never meant to hold; and (4) to walk out of his classroom bitter, wounded, and vengeful with no peace and no solutions.

Joseph was a person whom God Himself had transformed. Joseph's family mistreated him and sold him into slavery. In the end, however, Joseph viewed the entire situation through the lens of Christ. Instead of dwelling on the offense itself, he saw the purpose for what had happened and pointed others to do the same. He experienced restoration in his family. He experienced the peace of God.

> *"As for you, you meant evil against me, but God meant it for good in order to bring about this present result, to preserve many people alive."*
> *(Genesis 50:20)*

On the day the offense resurfaced in my mind, I realized what the enemy was after—and so did the Lord. As stated previously, the enemy wanted me to dwell on the hurt, while the Lord wanted me to remember the lesson. For the lesson (the truths) God brought to my heart through that offense transformed me in a most amazing way. It brought freedom and deliverance in how I handle matters moving forward.

Whatever offense you are holding onto today, release it—as well as the offender—into the loving hands of Jesus. Walk into His classroom, fall on bended knees, and allow the Lord to guide you and transform your life. Refuse to allow the offense and the offender to mold you. Instead, allow the Teacher Himself to transform you. He loves you so much.

> *Bless those who persecute you; bless and do not curse. Rejoice with those who rejoice, and weep with those who weep. Be of the same mind toward one another; do not be haughty in mind, but associate with the lowly. Do not be wise in your own estimation. Never pay back evil for evil to anyone. Respect what is right in the sight of all men. If possible, so far as it depends on you, be at peace with all men. Never take your own revenge, beloved, but leave room for the wrath of God, for it is written, "VENGEANCE IS MINE, I WILL REPAY," says the Lord. "BUT IF YOUR ENEMY IS HUNGRY, FEED HIM, AND IF HE IS THIRSTY, GIVE HIM A DRINK; FOR IN SO DOING YOU WILL HEAP BURNING COALS ON HIS HEAD." Do not be overcome by evil, but overcome evil with good.*
> *(Romans 12:14-21)*

Lord, please help me . . .

Lord, please help me . . .

Therefore if you have been raised up with Christ, keep seeking the things above, where Christ is, seated at the right hand of God. Set your mind on the things above, not on the things that are on earth.
—Colossians 3:1-2

I found myself repeatedly pondering over a situation, which the enemy was using to thwart my focus away from Jesus. As I sought the Lord for help, He began to speak to me about the importance of focusing on Him instead of on the problem. As He led me to His Word, I was truly moved by a particular passage. It was the story of a king, a message, a response, and a prayer.

Then some came and reported to Jehoshaphat, saying, "A great multitude is coming against you from beyond the sea, out of Aram and behold, they are in Hazazon-tamar (that is Engedi)." Jehoshaphat was afraid and turned his attention to seek the Lord, and proclaimed a fast throughout all Judah. So Judah gathered

> *together to seek help from the Lord; they even came*
> *from all the cities of Judah to seek the Lord.*
> *(2 Chronicles 20:2-4)*

Jehoshaphat, King of Judah, had received news that a great multitude was coming against him, and he became afraid. Yet instead of allowing fear to guide him, he allowed his faith in God to redirect his focus. Instead of setting his thoughts on the enemies, Jehoshaphat turned his attention to seek the only One who could help. As Jehoshaphat prayed, He reminded the Lord of His goodness, of His power, and of His past victories and promises. He also conversed with the Lord about the problem at hand (vv. 4-13). Then with great transparency and faith, Jehoshaphat prayed the following:

> *"O our God, will You not judge them? For we are*
> *powerless before this great multitude who are coming*
> *against us; nor do we know what to do, but our eyes*
> *are on You."*
> *(2 Chronicles 20:12)*

Jehoshaphat concluded his prayer with a powerful declaration, for the King knew they were powerless against the enemies and was uncertain as to what to do. However, he was confident in where their focus would be as they waited on God to act on their behalf.

As all of Judah stood before the Lord, awaiting His help, the following message was delivered:

> *Then in the midst of the assembly the Spirit of*
> *the Lord came upon Jahaziel the son of Zechariah, the*
> *son of Benaiah, the son of Jeiel, the son of Mattaniah,*
> *the Levite of the sons of Asaph; and he said, "Listen,*
> *all Judah and the inhabitants of Jerusalem and King*
> *Jehoshaphat: thus says the Lord to you, 'Do not fear*

> *or be dismayed because of this great multitude, for the battle is not yours but God's. Tomorrow go down against them. Behold, they will come up by the ascent of Ziz, and you will find them at the end of the valley in front of the wilderness of Jeruel. You need not fight in this battle; station yourselves, stand and see the salvation of the Lord on your behalf, O Judah and Jerusalem.' Do not fear or be dismayed; tomorrow go out to face them, for the Lord is with you."*
> *(2 Chronicles 20:14-17)*

God intervened on behalf of His people, and, my friend, He will do the same for you. When we turn our attention to seek the Lord, we will experience God's intervention as well as a peace that surpasses all understanding (Philippians 4:6-8).

What is holding your attention currently? What are you pondering the most? Instead of allowing the enemy, the problem, or the trial to command your thoughts, turn your heart to seek the Lord. For when you allow the scene in front of you (the hardships or circumstances) to speak louder to you than God's truth, worry and fear will result instead of God's peace.

Remember, just like Jehoshaphat, you too may feel powerless and uncertain as to how to manage your current situation. However, God sees the bigger picture. He sees what we are unable to view and promises to cause all things to work together for those who love Him (Romans 8:28). Turn your attention to seek the Lord, and keep your eyes upon Him. For He will be faithful to His own.

Lord, please help me . . .

*As a result of this many of His disciples withdrew and were not walking
with Him anymore. So Jesus said to the twelve, "You do not want to go
away also, do you?"*
—John 6:66-67

God is bringing all of His children to their very own personal
Promised Land—a place where He has assigned us to work and
carry out His kingdom agenda. However, while journeying toward these
ordained places, seasons may occur in which we find ourselves traveling
alone—not aloof from God but from those to whom we wished would
have accompanied us. The question is, will we allow these moments to
halt us in our journeys, or will we continue to follow Jesus?

David was the king of Israel, both blessed and anointed. Yet on one
particular day, David found himself fleeing for his life—not from an
enemy or even a stranger but from Absalom, his very own son. David
had to leave behind his home, his throne, and all that he loved.

*Then a messenger came to David, saying, "The hearts
of the men of Israel are with Absalom." David said*

> *to all his servants who were with him at Jerusalem,*
> *"Arise and let us flee, for otherwise none of us will*
> *escape from Absalom. Go in haste, or he will overtake*
> *us quickly and bring down calamity on us and strike*
> *the city with the edge of the sword." Then the king's*
> *servants said to the king, "Behold, your servants are*
> *ready to do whatever my lord the king chooses." So*
> *the king went out and all his household with him.*
> *But the king left ten concubines to keep the house. The*
> *king went out and all the people with him, and they*
> *stopped at the last house. Now all his servants passed*
> *on beside him, all the Cherethites, all the Pelethites*
> *and all the Gittites, six hundred men who had*
> *come with him from Gath, passed on before the king.*
> *(2 Samuel 15:13-18)*

We all have experienced periods in our lives when people who we trusted and loved rejected and betrayed us. We have also experienced times when God had to step in and purposefully remove particular acquaintances from our lives who were unsafe or unhealthy. Looking back at my own journey, those times were some of the hardest to get through. However, today I can truthfully say they were most necessary.

Remember:

1. *Not all people will stand by you* when the going gets tough. Indeed, some may walk away. But when this happens, you must move on with Jesus. Do not allow any bitterness to take root in your soul. What you may deem as rejection may literally be God's protection. Move on with Jesus, even though others may turn away.

2. *Not all people will believe in your dream,* your calling, or even the mission God has called you to undertake. Do not get stuck looking over your shoulder, desiring certain individuals to believe in you or to join you in your work. Keep moving on with Jesus. Never make it your life's mission to attempt to force people to believe in you or to be a part of what God has called you to do. Trust the

Lord to place in your life the people He wants to help you, encourage you, and be involved with what He is calling you to do. Stop casting your pearls before swine.

3. *God sees the bigger picture.* A purpose exists in what you are going through. God knows what He is going to do in and through the circumstances He is allowing in your life. Even those betrayals and rejections He will use to make you more like His Son, Jesus. Trust Him; He will bring beauty from ashes.

At a time when David needed support and encouragement the most, people fled. However, God did not. Through it all, David trusted in the Lord. David allowed his brokenness to drive him to the Lord, moving forward with Him. David entrusted to God the kingdom from which he had fled, the people who had betrayed him, and the outcome of what God would do through it all.

What did David learn through this difficult time? We read about it in Psalm 3.

> *O Lord, how my adversaries have increased!*
> *Many are rising up against me.*
> *Many are saying of my soul,*
> *"There is no deliverance for him in God." Selah.*
> *But You, O Lord, are a shield about me,*
> *My glory, and the One who lifts my head.*
> *I was crying to the Lord with my voice,*
> *And He answered me from His holy mountain. Selah.*
> *I lay down and slept;*
> *I awoke, for the Lord sustains me.*
> *I will not be afraid of ten thousands of people*
> *Who have set themselves against me round about.*
> *Arise, O Lord; save me, O my God!*
> *For You have smitten all my enemies on the cheek;*
> *You have shattered the teeth of the wicked.*
> *Salvation belongs to the Lord;*
> *Your blessing be upon Your people! Selah.*
> *(Psalm 3:1-8)*

David understood that God was his shield, his glory, and the One who lifted his head. He also understood that God was faithful while others proved faithless. The same holds true for us today. Not everyone will be for you or stand by you. However, God will.

Always.

At the end of the day, that is all that should ever matter.

> **Simon Peter answered Him, "Lord, to whom shall we go? You have words of eternal life. We have believed and have come to know that You are the Holy One of God."**
> **(John 6:68-69)**

"Though none go with me, I still will follow."[2]

Lord, please help me . . .

____

____

____

____

____

____

---

2. Simon Marak, "I Have Decided to Follow Jesus," presumed to have originally been written around 1935. Public domain.

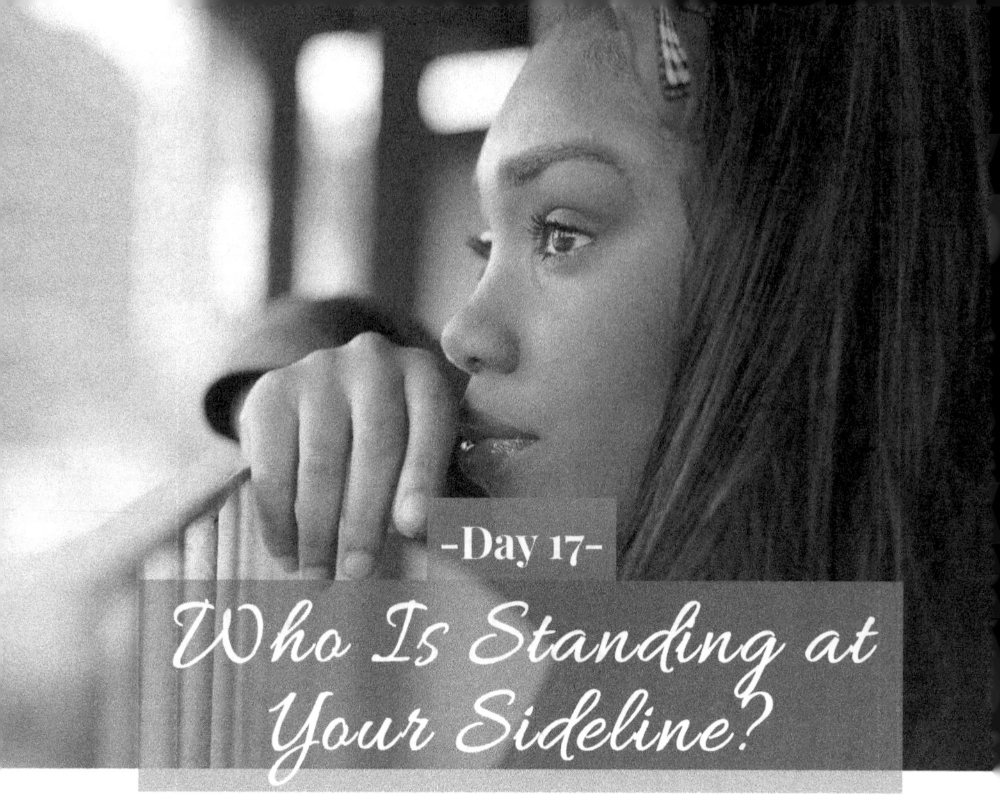

Who Is Standing at Your Sideline?

Therefore let us draw near with confidence to the throne of grace, so that we may receive mercy and find grace to help in time of need.
—Hebrews 4:16

On January 14, 2020, millions watched as Clemson and LSU played for the College Football Playoff National Championship. Excitement filled the air as both teams took to the field to compete in one of the biggest televised events of the year. As the game commenced, numerous life lessons began to emerge from a hundred-yard classroom called a *football field*.

In every football game, plays are executed that result in both positive and negative outcomes. Flags are thrown, time-outs are called, and mistakes are made. Yet these moments create opportunities for players, coaches, and fans to respond either positively or negatively to the results.

With only a few minutes remaining in the game, Clemson's quarterback, Trevor Lawrence, fumbled the ball. As the entire nation watched, the young man made his way to the sideline where Clemson's head coach stood watching and waiting. How Coach Dabo Swinney responded to the young man's fumble will forever be remembered in the hearts of many—especially in the heart of one young man standing on that sideline.

As reporters filled the room for the post-game interview, Swinney took his seat. Correspondents prepared to ask their specific questions to the coach, and one particular inquiry immediately grabbed my attention. In regard to Lawrence's fumble, one reporter was curious to know what the coach had to say to the young man as he approached the sideline. The reporter asked, "What did you tell him?" Swinney responded, "I just told him to keep his head up. I told him that I loved him, and this was a great opportunity to lead and to respond."

The coach placed more value on Lawrence's life than on his fumble. He did not look outwardly to the mistake but inwardly to the young man's heart. Swinney immediately sought to encourage Lawrence, reinforcing his belief in the young man by reminding him that he was loved. He pointed the young man toward the opportunity that was in front of him, instead of focusing on the fumble that was behind him. The coach conveyed encouraging words that built Lawrence up, instead of damaging ones intended to tear him down. Swinney pointed others to the good in the young man's life, to his many accomplishments, and to his character. The coach expressed his confidence in the young man by stating, "I wouldn't trade him for anybody."

Consider Jesus as the greatest sideline Coach of all time. Throughout the Bible, we read of countless individuals who found themselves standing at a sideline with Jesus. Well, maybe not a hundred-yard sideline, but a life-altering moment type of sideline—a moment where grace was desperately needed and mercy was begged for. As we take a quick glance at some familiar stories from God's Word, note how Jesus placed more value and emphasis on people's lives and their callings than He did on their mistakes.

- Peter denied Christ at a most crucial time.
- David, a man after God's own heart, dove headfirst into an adulterous relationship, then murder, then fleeing from the God who had loved him and had led him throughout all his life.
- Jonah ran from God's calling on his life.

At one time or another, we have all found ourselves standing at a sideline with Jesus, in need of His mercy and His grace. From fumbles to poor decisions, we have knelt on bended knees, pleading for God to forgive us, restore us, and even grant us a new beginning or a restored relationship. And during such moments, Jesus met us there with both mercy and grace.

We can certainly learn valuable lessons from Coach Dabo Swinney about dealing with those standing at our sidelines. However, more importantly, we can learn from Jesus. For no one will ever teach or conform a heart like our Savior.

Who is standing at your sideline right now? Who has blown it with you? Who needs your grace, your mercy? A second chance? May we never cease to give what has been given to us over and over by our Savior: love, forgiveness, mercy, and grace.

> *Treat others the same way you want them to treat you.*
> *(Luke 6:31)*
>
> *Be merciful, just as your Father is merciful.*
> *(Luke 6:36)*

Lord, please help me . . .

____

____

____

____

____

____

____

____

____

____

Abram journeyed on, continuing toward the Negev.
—Genesis 12:9

I n Genesis 12, God called Abram to "go forth" from his family, his country, and his father's house to the land the Lord would show him. According to God's Word, Abram obeyed the voice of God and moved forward.

> *Now the LORD said to Abram,*
> *"Go forth from your country,*
> *And from your relatives*
> *And from your father's house,*
> *To the land which I will show you;*
> *And I will make you a great nation,*
> *And I will bless you,*
> *And make your name great;*
> *And so you shall be a blessing;*
> *And I will bless those who bless you,*

> *And the one who curses you I will curse.*
> *And in you all the families of the earth will be blessed."*
> *So Abram went forth as the* LORD *had spoken to*
> *him; and Lot went with him. Now Abram was*
> *seventy-five years old when he departed from Haran.*
> *Abram took Sarai his wife and Lot his nephew, and*
> *all their possessions which they had accumulated,*
> *and the persons which they had acquired in Haran,*
> *and they set out for the land of Canaan; thus*
> *they came to the land of Canaan. Abram passed*
> *through the land as far as the site of Shechem, to*
> *the oak of Moreh. Now the Canaanite was then in*
> *the land. The* LORD *appeared to Abram and said,*
> *"To your descendants I will give this land." So he*
> *built an altar there to the* LORD *who had appeared*
> *to him. Then he proceeded from there to the*
> *mountain on the east of Bethel, and pitched his tent,*
> *with Bethel on the west and Ai on the east; and there*
> *he built an altar to the* LORD *and called upon the*
> *name of the* LORD. *Abram journeyed on, continuing*
> *toward the Negev.*
> *(Genesis 12:1-9)*

As I was reading this particular passage, one verse gripped my heart: "Abram *journeyed on, continuing toward* the Negev" (v. 9). This message has continued to move my spirit, especially through times of studying the Word of God and praying: *Move forward with Jesus, and do what He has called you to do.* Another related message I pondered from Joshua 3 was "setting out and going after it." What does all this entail for my life? "Journeying on, continuing toward" what God has called and ordained for me to do.

Because of the effects of our journeys, one of the hardest things to do at times is just that—"continuing." To "journey on" when we are weak and tired can be most trying. Because of the effects of the trial, we often allow ourselves to be blinded to a future and deceived into thinking we are not "continuing toward" anything at all. Yet, you and I both know who the deceiver of such thinking is.

> *We are destroying speculations and every lofty thing raised up against the knowledge of God, and we are taking every thought captive to the obedience of Christ.*
> *(2 Corinthians 10:5)*

I also believe we have all come to a point in our lives when we are "journeying on" but not "continuing toward" what God has called us to do. We have either become complacent, possibly even stuck, or we are not surrendered to God's calling upon our lives.

In order for Abram to have lived out his divine calling, he had to "journey on" while "continuing toward," in spite of the many hardships he faced along the way. My friend, we too must do the same. I have found myself praying repeatedly, *Lord, do not let me miss it.* I want to "journey on" while "continuing toward" the path on which God wants me to travel and the calling He wants me to carry out for His glory and kingdom building. With all my heart, I want to do the thing He wants me to do.

People are waiting on the other side of your "yes" to God—people who will be impacted by your testimony, your gifts, your talents, and the influence you will have on their lives through Christ Jesus. "Journey on," my friends, while "continuing toward" what God is calling you to do. Do not shrink back; do not give up! Guard against becoming complacent. Move forward with Jesus.

Lord, please help me . . .

Consider it all joy, my brethren, when you encounter various trials, knowing that the testing of your faith produces endurance. And let endurance have its perfect result, so that you may be perfect and complete, lacking in nothing.
—James 1:2-4

Throughout our journey as Christians, we will face periods of suffering from trials in our lives. These encounters will, at times, produce stressful moments adjacent with fear within the hearts of believers. Yet instead of running to the throne room of grace, we often rush to other resources for help and comfort, ones that demand self-defense and self-strategy.

We panic.
We plan.
We pursue.
We protect.

First: At times, we panic. The trial that has aggressively come often produces fear. If we are not careful, we will immediately give power to the forbidding panic. But God's Word says,

> *"Peace I leave with you; My peace I give to you; not as the world gives do I give to you. Do not let your heart be troubled, nor let it be fearful."*
> *(John 14:27)*

Second: At times, we plan. In the mix of the brewing trial, we instantly try to figure out the best way to manage the hardship at hand. How? We strategize. We pull out a piece of paper, spread it out on the table, and devise our own blueprint plan. We look around at the best options possible to handle the crisis. But God's Word says,

> *Many plans are in a man's heart,*
> *But the counsel of the LORD WILL STAND.*
> *(Proverbs 19:21)*
>
> *"For My thoughts are not your thoughts,*
> *Nor are your ways My ways," declares the LORD.*
> *"FOR AS the heavens are higher than the earth,*
> *So are My ways higher than your ways*
> *And My thoughts than your thoughts."*
> *(Isaiah 55:8-9)*

Third: At times, we pursue. After we carefully plan our course of action, we pursue it with all our might. Then, as we are running speedily ahead, we look back, as if to motion for God to *join us* in our plans. But God's Word says,

> *There is a way which seems right to a man,*
> *But its end is the way of death.*
> *(Proverbs 14:12)*
>
> *The mind of man plans his way,*
> *But the LORD DIRECTS HIS STEPS.*
> *(PROVERBS 16:9)*

Fourth: At times, we try to protect. When the trials hit our lives, our first line of defense may be one of self-preservation. We try to guard ourselves from suffering, attempting to get out of the trial at hand. However, this only hinders God's work in our lives. We try to protect and defend ourselves, especially against enemy attacks. We want to safeguard our reputation. We want to shield our hearts from being hurt any further, so we build walls. Yet we must remember this important truth: God will avenge His own. We can both rest in His love and faithfulness while trusting Him to intervene as only He can on our behalf. God's Word says,

> *"No weapon that is formed against you will prosper;*
> *And every tongue that accuses you in judgment you*
> *will condemn.*
> *This is the heritage of the servants of the* LORD,
> *And their vindication is from Me," declares the* LORD.
> *(Isaiah 54:17)*
>
> *The* LORD IS FOR ME; *I* WILL NOT FEAR;
> *What can man do to me?*
> *The* LORD IS FOR ME AMONG THOSE WHO HELP ME;
> *Therefore I will look with satisfaction on those who*
> *hate me.*
> *(Psalm 118:6-7)*

So how do we deal with trials? First, we submit the crises, as well as our lives, to the Lord. Doing so will allow Him to work unhinderedly, producing peace within our hearts, whereas submitting to the trial itself and allowing our lives to be molded and shaped by it will harvest fear and anxiety within.

Second, we pray to see the trial through the eyes of Jesus instead of through our own lens. The Lord sees the bigger picture, while we only see what's in front of us. Therefore, we can trust Him with what we can't see or even understand. We pray for strength and the grace to walk through the trial, knowing God is with us, while submitting daily to His Word and obeying His truth.

Third, we trust God to bring about the result that He wants from the trial. Our current circumstance is not just some random occurrence; it is our assignment. And within that assignment is a purpose and a plan to make us more like Jesus. For God is working out of us what needs to go, while building in us what needs to be developed or strengthened.

In the book of James, we are told to "consider it all joy" when encountering various trials. So instead of panicking, planning, pursuing, and protecting, submit it all to God. Pray to see the trial through His eyes, and trust him to bring about the result He is after through the time of hardship. Stay in His Word, be obedient to what He tells you to do, and continue to be faithful in prayer. He hears you and is working even now on your behalf. Don't give up.

Lord, please help me . . .

____

____

____

____

____

____

____

Without consultation, plans are frustrated,
But with many counselors they succeed.
—Proverbs 15:22

H ave you ever sought advice from people you were close to? Certainly, we all have. In so doing, there are several important things to consider, such as ensuring the counsel we seek comes from those we can both learn from and pass along lessons from to others with confidence. But there is one very critical step we must take before we seek guidance from anyone. . . .

Before going to others, go to God first. Does the Bible encourage us to seek godly counsel? Yes! Proverbs 15:22 states,

Without consultation, plans are frustrated,
But with many counselors they succeed.

However, before pursuing human guidance, we must first beseech the Lord. He is the wisdom that we need, and He holds the answers we desperately seek. He promises to guide us with His eye upon us (Psalm 32:8).

Allow me to share some tips in seeking godly counsel. First, make sure he or she (1) demonstrates true godly character, (2) is faithfully in the Word, (3) is a prayer warrior, and (4) demonstrates the fruits of the Spirit. Second, filter any advice through the Word of God. If the advice being offered to you contradicts the Word of God, you know instantly it is not from God. It is imperative that we faithfully study the Word in order to know His truth. His Word must always trump that of man's opinion (John 8:31-32). God's will, will prevail over great ideas. Excitement over new dreams can be contagious, so much so that we may find ourselves saying to another, "That idea sounds great. Do it!" However, this does not necessarily mean it was of the Lord. David, a man after God's own heart, wanted to build a house for the Lord. When he shared his desire with Nathan, God's prophet, instantly Nathan offered David counsel in the matter. He stated, in 2 Samuel 7:3, "Go, do all that is in your mind, for the LORD is with you." However, Nathan's guidance was *not* of the Lord. It was not God's plan for David to build Him a house, for God had another individual in mind to carry out the mission. He did, however, allow David to help.

Third, while filtering through the Word of God, you must simultaneously place before the Lord the counsel given to you through periods of prayer. If you sense a restlessness within, take heed. Even godly people can get it wrong. At one time, I was seeking God for a decision. As I was praying, I went to three different individuals for counsel to which all three gave different guidance. Yet when I went to God, He made clear through His Word and through a time of prayer what His will for my life was. View the counsel you are given through the lens of prayer.

And fourth, when God gives you an answer, obey what He is telling you to do. Whether it is through a time of waiting or taking a step to move forward, do the next thing God tells you to do.

I want to leave you with some final cautions:

1. There will be people who will not want to see good come your way. Avoid such persons when seeking counsel

2. Not everyone you go to will understand God's call on your life or even the work He is doing through you. As a result, their counsel will reflect such assessment. Don't be discouraged; God has the final say in what He is calling you to do.

3. Yes, go to Christians for godly counsel; however, just because someone has a particular standing in the community, or even the local church, as a Christian, does not mean they live at the feet of Jesus. Be cautious (see tip number one).

4. Always make God's Word the standard by which you measure any advice given to you.

5. Avoid, at all costs, going to those given to gossip for counsel. No, no, no!

6. Trust God. You will not miss His best when you seek Him first.

Surround yourself with wise counsel, and listen and obey what He tells you to do.

Lord, please help me . . .

*So she departed and went and gleaned in the field after the reapers;
and she happened to come to the portion of the field belonging to Boaz,
who was of the family of Elimelech.*
—Ruth 2:3

Due to a famine, Naomi and her husband left Bethlehem and journeyed to the land of Moab. While there, Naomi's husband died, and later her two sons died. Grieving the loss of her family, and upon hearing the news that the famine was now over in Bethlehem, Naomi made the decision to return home. As she attempted to say goodbye to both of her daughters-in-law, Orpah made the decision to stay with her family, but Ruth was determined to follow Naomi, leaving behind all she had ever known. After Naomi recognized Ruth's determination, they both set out for Bethlehem.

Naomi and Ruth returned to Bethlehem during barley harvest. Realizing the need for food, Ruth made a request of her mother-in-law. Yet unbeknownst to Ruth, God had a bigger plan in her request than she ever could have fathomed.

And Ruth the Moabitess said to Naomi, "Please let me go to the field and glean among the ears of grain after one in whose sight I may find favor." And she said to her, "Go, my daughter." So she departed and went and gleaned in the field after the reapers; and she happened to come to the portion of the field belonging to Boaz, who was of the family of Elimelech.
(Ruth 2:2-3)

Of all the fields Ruth could have come to, she came to a portion in which God had specifically ordained her to be. Amid this field, Ruth received both provision and protection. In addition, a God-ordained meeting occurred—one which she was ushered into and through which God's plan would unfold.

Ruth's arrival to the field caught the attention of Boaz, thus prompting him to ask, "Whose young woman is this?" As Boaz learned of Ruth's loyalty to her mother-in-law, and of her departure from her own family, he was captivated by her character, impressed by her work ethic, and inspired to help. Further, he was prompted to protect her by encouraging her not to go to another field.

Then Boaz said to Ruth, "Listen carefully, my daughter. Do not go to glean in another field; furthermore, do not go on from this one, but stay here with my maids. Let your eyes be on the field which they reap, and go after them. Indeed, I have commanded the servants not to touch you. When you are thirsty, go to the water jars and drink from what the servants draw." Then she fell on her face, bowing to the ground and said to him, "Why have I found favor in your sight that you should take notice of me, since I am a foreigner?" Boaz replied to her, "All that you have done for your mother-in-law after the death of your husband has been fully reported to me, and how you left your father and your mother and the land of your birth, and came

> *to a people that you did not previously know. May the Lord reward your work, and your wages be full from the Lord, the God of Israel, under whose wings you have come to seek refuge."*
> *(Ruth 2:8-12)*

Through God's gracious leading, Boaz extended his kindness to Ruth by giving her food and providing extra grain for her to take home to her mother-in-law. His kindness was also extended by his willingness to protect her and by encouraging her to stay in the field with his reapers. When Ruth returned home, Naomi was so moved by what had taken place, and she was blessed to have food as well. She posed a question to Ruth, then encouraged her not to leave the field to which she had come.

> *Her mother-in-law then said to her, "Where did you glean today and where did you work? May he who took notice of you be blessed." So she told her mother-in-law with whom she had worked and said, "The name of the man with whom I worked today is Boaz." Naomi said to her daughter-in-law, "May he be blessed of the Lord who has not withdrawn his kindness to the living and to the dead." Again Naomi said to her, "The man is our relative, he is one of our closest relatives." Then Ruth the Moabitess said, "Furthermore, he said to me, 'You should stay close to my servants until they have finished all my harvest.'" Naomi said to Ruth, her daughter-in-law, "It is good, my daughter, that you go out with his maids, so that others do not fall upon you in another field." So she stayed close by the maids of Boaz in order to glean until the end of the barley harvest and the wheat harvest. And she lived with her mother-in-law.*
> *(Ruth 2:19-23)*

God's plans for both Ruth and Naomi exceeded their own expectations. As they had previously walked in despair due to their devastating losses, they one day found themselves walking in hope due to God's faithfulness.

So often amid pain, it is difficult to envision any good that can come out of it. While Ruth saw the loss, God saw the redemption. While Naomi perceived God's hand as being against her, God knew His hand was for her. While Ruth and Naomi feared provision, God saw a portion of a field awaiting Ruth's entrance, where not only provision would be waiting but where a plan would be carried out—a plan involving a marriage, a child, a lineage, and a Redeemer. God always sees the bigger picture. He sees what we cannot.

> *So Boaz took Ruth, and she became his wife, and he went in to her. And the Lord enabled her to conceive, and she gave birth to a son. Then the women said to Naomi, "Blessed is the Lord who has not left you without a redeemer today, and may his name become famous in Israel. May he also be to you a restorer of life and a sustainer of your old age; for your daughter-in-law, who loves you and is better to you than seven sons, has given birth to him." Then Naomi took the child and laid him in her lap, and became his nurse. The neighbor women gave him a name, saying, "A son has been born to Naomi!" So they named him Obed. He is the father of Jesse, the father of David.*
> *(Ruth 4:13-17)*

God wants you in a portion of a field. Are you in it? If so, cease from gazing at another field. For where God has you is where He will provide for you, protect you, comfort you, and unfold His plan for you. Do not lose hope—God sees you and is working even now on your behalf. Stay in the field.

Lord, please help me . . .

Please Stay on the Wall; Someone Needs You

So I sent messengers to them, saying, "I am doing a great work and I cannot come down. Why should the work stop while I leave it and come down to you?"
—Nehemiah 6:3

Tom had reached out to a friend for prayer. As he conveyed his request, the individual began to pray over his need. When the prayer concluded, Tom humbly stated, "Please stay on the wall."

Tom understood the effectiveness of the Christian who tirelessly commits himself to sharing the gospel of Christ. In that same token, Tom knew all too well the intense desire of the enemy to deter the Christian from staying on the wall through various means (e.g., discouragement and weariness). Tom knew that for people to be reached, including himself, Christians must stay on the wall instead of climbing down and walking away from a God-called mission.

Years prior, an urgent need touched the heart of a man named Nehemiah. God used the hardship to move Nehemiah not only to a period of prayer but to one of action as well.

> *The words of Nehemiah the son of Hacaliah.*
> *Now it happened in the month Chislev, in the*
> *twentieth year, while I was in Susa*
> *the capitol, that Hanani, one of my brothers,*
> *and some men from Judah came; and I asked them*
> *concerning the Jews who had escaped and had*
> *survived the captivity, and about Jerusalem. They*
> *said to me, "The remnant there in the province*
> *who survived the captivity are in great distress*
> *and reproach, and the wall of Jerusalem is broken*
> *down and its gates are burned with fire."*
> *When I heard these words, I sat down and wept and*
> *mourned for days; and I was fasting and praying*
> *before the God of heaven.*
> *(Nehemiah 1:1-4)*

Not only were the people discouraged, but they were in danger. Why? Because the walls that had once surrounded and protected them were now broken down. The walls needed to be rebuilt, and God called Nehemiah to the special task of rebuilding.

As Nehemiah embarked on the mission God had called him to, fierce enemies often met him on the path. Continuously, the adversaries came with snarling remarks and fearful tactics. Their goal? To get Nehemiah and the people to cease work on the walls.

> *Now when it was reported to Sanballat, Tobiah, to*
> *Geshem the Arab and to the rest of our enemies that*
> *I had rebuilt the wall, and that no breach remained*
> *in it, although at that time I had not set up the*
> *doors in the gates, then Sanballat and Geshem sent a*
> *message to me, saying, "Come, let us meet together*
> *at Chephirim in the plain of Ono." But they were*
> *planning to harm me. So I sent messengers to them,*
> *saying, "I am doing a great work and I cannot come*
> *down. Why should the work stop while I leave it and*
> *come down to you?"*
> *(Nehemiah 6:1-3).*

Notice once more Nehemiah's response to the ongoing threats of the enemy:

1. Nehemiah *focused* on the mission at hand: "I am doing a great work." He knew what he had been called to do and why he had been called to do it. He recognized who it was that had called him to the work, and this caused him to spotlight the labor as one of greatness.

2. Nehemiah recognized the importance of the wall and its benefit to others: "I cannot come down." Nehemiah's words, "I cannot come down," reflected the heart of a man who knew that his mission was not about himself but instead about the need for others' safety and protection. Nehemiah comprehended the importance and the benefit of the wall being rebuilt. Furthermore, Nehemiah was called to act courageously with great perseverance to see the wall to completion.

3. Nehemiah *remembered* his calling (giving allegiance to God), *rebuffed* the enemies (by not giving them power), *remained* steadfast (continuing the work), and *refused* to leave his post (standing firmly in his position), even in the midst of opposition: "Why should the work stop while I leave it and come down to you?"

Every single day we are given to live, we have an opportunity to impact others for the kingdom. In so doing, we can either stay on the wall, carrying out the work God has called us to, or we can allow discouragement and criticism from the enemy to talk us down from the wall God has assigned to us.

May I encourage all of us today to do the following: First, refuse to lose our focus. Remember, for such a time as this, we have been called to do the task in front of us. Focus on Jesus instead of on the problems. Second, recognize the importance of what God has called us to do. Third, remember our calling (giving allegiance to God), rebuff the enemies (by not giving them power), remain steadfast (continuing the work), and refuse to leave our post (standing firmly in our positions), even amidst opposition.

Onward, soldiers! Someone needs you. Please stay on the wall.

Lord, please help me . . .

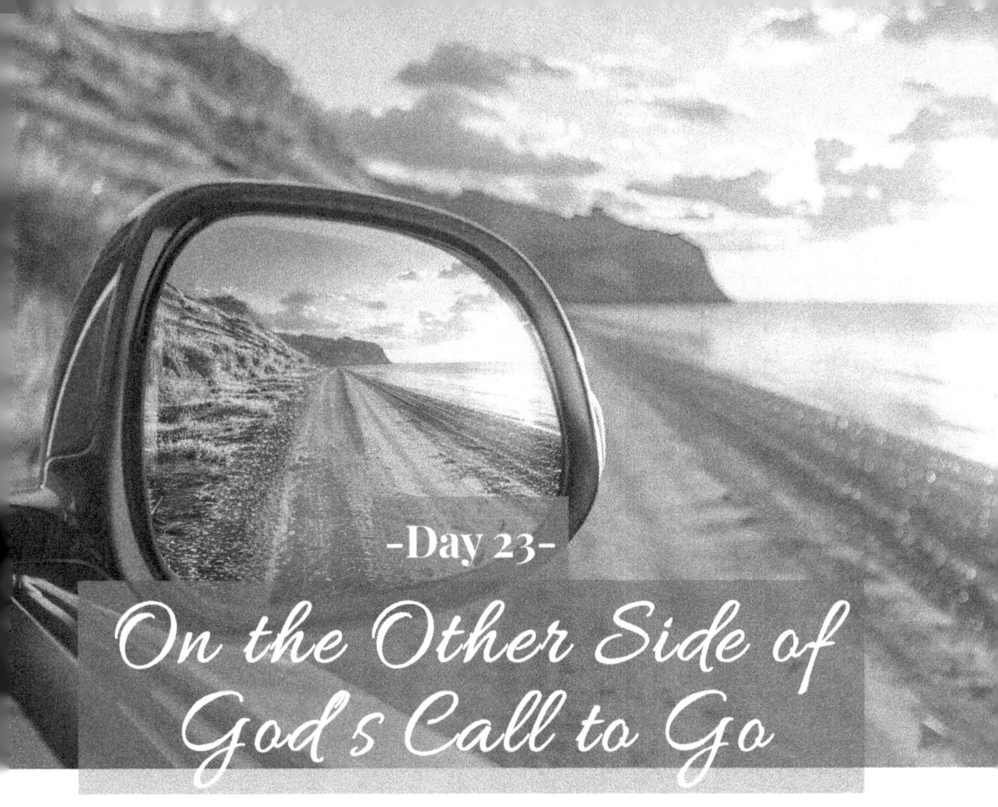

"Behold, I will do something new,
Now it will spring forth;
Will you not be aware of it?
I will even make a roadway in the wilderness,
Rivers in the desert."
—Isaiah 43:19

While dialoguing over their yesterdays with family and friends, most all have heard the expression, "Back in the day." This expression usually precedes an introduction to a story of former times with enjoyable memories. As of late, I have found myself pondering over this phrase, while returning to dwellings and certain eras in my life.

Recently I had the opportunity to travel home to visit family. One day I was sitting in my mother's den, watching both her and my sister go through picture albums. Narratives began to unravel as they reminisced on days gone by. While they did this, I sat quietly, pondering over my own past.

Later in the day, I traveled to see additional family members in a different part of town. As I was driving past familiar locations, I found myself reminiscing on those "back-in-the-day" periods and places that had marked my life in some form or fashion. One road led me to a parking lot of a once-familiar dwelling, and a rush of thanksgiving flooded my soul for how God had grown me during those seasons of my life. I drove by a mentor's home where God had used a precious widow to teach me His ways. On another road, I visited with a dear woman in her front yard who had meant so much to my family and who loved Jesus more than anyone I had ever met.

All of those memories of dreams I had once cultivated, fun times I had shared with friends, and detours I wished I had never taken, made my heart begin to stir with a deep awareness and thankfulness for all that God had done in my life over the years and where He had brought me.

I have often witnessed people who long for those days of old and even wish they could go back. I, on the other hand, am not one of those individuals. That was then, and this is now. "Behold, I will do something new. . . ." The place, the period, and the season God has brought me to currently has served as one of the most wonderful periods of my life.

I love the story of Ruth. As stated in a previous devotion, after suffering a great loss, Ruth left behind everything she had ever known—family, friends, and a home—to follow her mother-in-law to an unfamiliar place. She embraced a new future instead of holding on to her past. Ruth never could have envisioned all the blessings that awaited her as God orchestrated her steps to a field where she would be noticed, protected, and provided for by a man named Boaz. Later, she was united in marriage with Boaz and blessed with a beautiful child.

> *But Ruth said, "Do not urge me to leave you or turn back from following you; for where you go, I will go, and where you lodge, I will lodge. Your people shall be my people, and your God, my God. Where you die, I will die, and there I will be buried. Thus*

> *may the Lord do to me, and worse, if anything*
> *but death parts you and me."*
> *(Ruth 1:16-17)*

Embracing the new thing God is doing in my life has not always been easy, but I can say with certainty that it has always been worth it. I never dreamed God would call this small-town girl to travel down the paths He has called me to travel. Yet I am so thankful He gave me the grace to answer His call. On the other side of God's call to go were blessings I never envisioned.

Oh, what I would have missed had I listened to my fears, my doubts, and even those voices attempting to thwart me from moving forward to the future destiny God had waiting for me. I want to share some important truths that I pray you and I will always remember:

1. Fear will sit you down and cause you to shrink back. But saying yes to the call of God will move you forward to your destiny.
2. Doubt will cause you to ride the waves of unbelief. Faith will keep you anchored.
3. Not everyone will understand the call of God on your life.
4. Not everyone will support you as you move forward to the new thing God is calling you to do—some from a lack of understanding and others from jealousy.
5. Not everyone will agree with your transplanting to a new place, and some may even cease their friendship with you.
6. *Remember this:* You and I will not stand before those everyones; rather, we will stand before God.
7. I learned early on to move forward with Jesus and leave those fears, those doubts, and those everyones to His care.
8. Though none go with me, I still will follow.

While journeying down roads previously traveled, we can enjoy those memories and those precious moments from our yesterdays. I will always hold dear my precious memories, but I pray to hold tighter to the hand of Jesus as He ushers me to move forward with Him wherever He leads. For on the other side of His call to go is where I long to be, more than sitting in those past boats, longing for days of old.

Lord, please help me . . .

____

____

____

____

____

____

____

____

____

Lord, please help me . . .

____

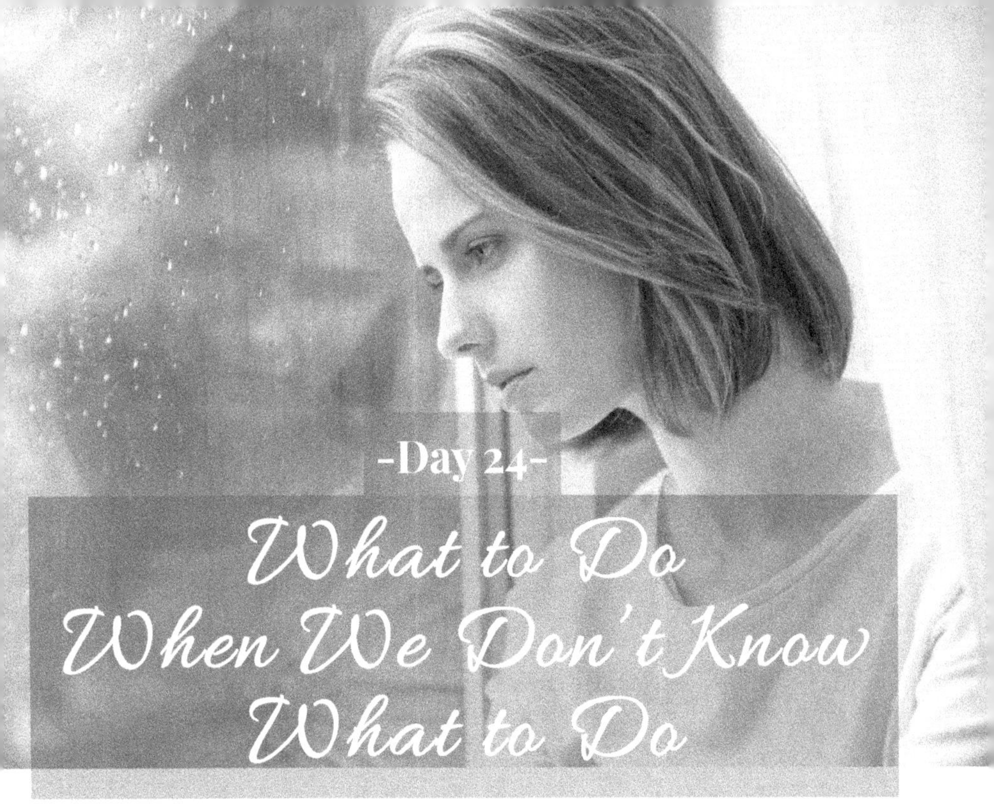

But seek first His kingdom and His righteousness, and all these things will be added to you.
—Matthew 6:33

Seminary life has been so wonderful to me. God has greatly blessed me, as I have enjoyed the many years I have lived in Texas. Years ago, as the educational journey began, my voyage seemed to be set as I pursued not only my master's degree but my doctoral degree as well. However, as the graduation date approached, so did a timeline for many decisions to be made. As a result, fear began to creep in due to clouds of uncertainties looming over my head. No personal blueprint plan would work. I literally had to put my plans down and seek God's will. For my plans were not the Lord's plans.

In looking back, I remember the tug-of-war I experienced when the door opened for me to move to Texas to attend seminary. I was perfectly happy in the place I was residing and was not looking to move. When the opportunity came to go to Texas, it was quite a surprise, to say the least. However, as I began to seek the Lord, through prayer and through His Word, He made clear to me that He had indeed opened the door for me to move.

On the other side of the Lord's open door awaited a purpose, a plan, and blessings I never envisioned. Had I allowed my plans to stand in the way—or even my emotions—I could have missed amazing opportunities waiting for me from God. It is important to note here, God was the one who opened the door. He was calling me to follow Him, whereas I had been so used to asking Him to follow my directional course. I am so glad I listened and followed His plan instead of my own.

Now, years later, I continue to walk in the blessings and purpose God has for my life. Yet now, once again, I am waiting on His direction for the next step of this journey. (These periods will come throughout our lives.) So what do we do when we do not know what to do? Well, I am glad you asked. I have learned some important truths I would like to entrust to you that God has shown me throughout the years, in times of waiting and in times of seeking.

We Seek Jesus

God says in His Word that He will show us the way to go.

> *I will instruct you and teach you in the way which you should go;*
> *I will counsel you with My eye upon you.*
> *(Psalm 32:8)*

Keep praying, keep asking, keep seeking.

> *Be anxious for nothing, but in everything by prayer and supplication with thanksgiving let your requests be made known to God. And the peace of God, which surpasses all comprehension, will guard your hearts and your minds in Christ Jesus.*
> *(Philippians 4:6-7)*

We Trust Him

We trust, knowing that God has a plan and that He will move on our behalf to bring it to fruition. We trust in His plan above our own.

Trust in the LORD with all your heart
And do not lean on your own understanding.
In all your ways acknowledge Him,
And He will make your paths straight.
(Proverbs 3:5-6)

We Wait

Before jumping ahead, wait on God's direction and answer. If He is silent, wait. If He has not made the direction clear, wait. For in His appointed time, He will act.

The LORD is good to those who wait for Him,
To the person who seeks Him.
(Lamentations 3:25)

I wait for the LORD, my soul does wait,
And in His word do I hope.
(Psalm 130:5)

For from days of old they have not heard or
perceived by ear,
Nor has the eye seen a God besides You,
Who acts on behalf of the one who waits for Him.
(Isaiah 64:4)

As you wait, enlist prayer partners to pray for you and with you.

We Rest in God

We are reminded in God's Word that our days were ordained by God before we were ever born. So we can rest in His sovereign plan and care for our lives. In Psalm 139, we read,

> *Your eyes have seen my unformed substance;*
> *And in Your book were all written*
> *The days that were ordained for me,*
> *When as yet there was not one of them.*
> *(Psalm 139:16)*

We are reminded that God will go before us, planting us where He wants us to be.

> *"Who goes before you on your way, to seek out a place for you to encamp, in fire by night and cloud by day, to show you the way in which you should go."*
> *(Deuteronomy 1:33)*
>
> *"See, I have placed the land before you; go in and possess the land which the LORD swore to give to your fathers, to Abraham, to Isaac, and to Jacob, to them and their descendants after them."*
> *(Deuteronomy 1:8)*

As you seek, trust, wait, and rest, also pay attention to the Lord's activity in your life. Just recently the Lord spoke to me in the form of direction by reminding me of what He is doing in my life for His kingdom purposes. It was not just one thing I was noticing; rather, it was several acts of His intervention, blessings, and movement—all pointing toward His calling upon my life. As I continued to watch and listen, I took heed to a message being spoken repeatedly to me through His Word and through my circumstances.

When God reveals the next step, be obedient to what He tells you to do, and move forward in faith and in total dependence upon Him, thanking Him for His faithfulness to you. Again, if God only reveals one step at a time, be obedient and take it. For that step will lead to the next step, and to the next step, and eventually to what God is calling you to do. He is and will always be faithful.

Lord, please help me . . .

____

____

____

____

____

____

____

____

Lord, please help me . . .

____

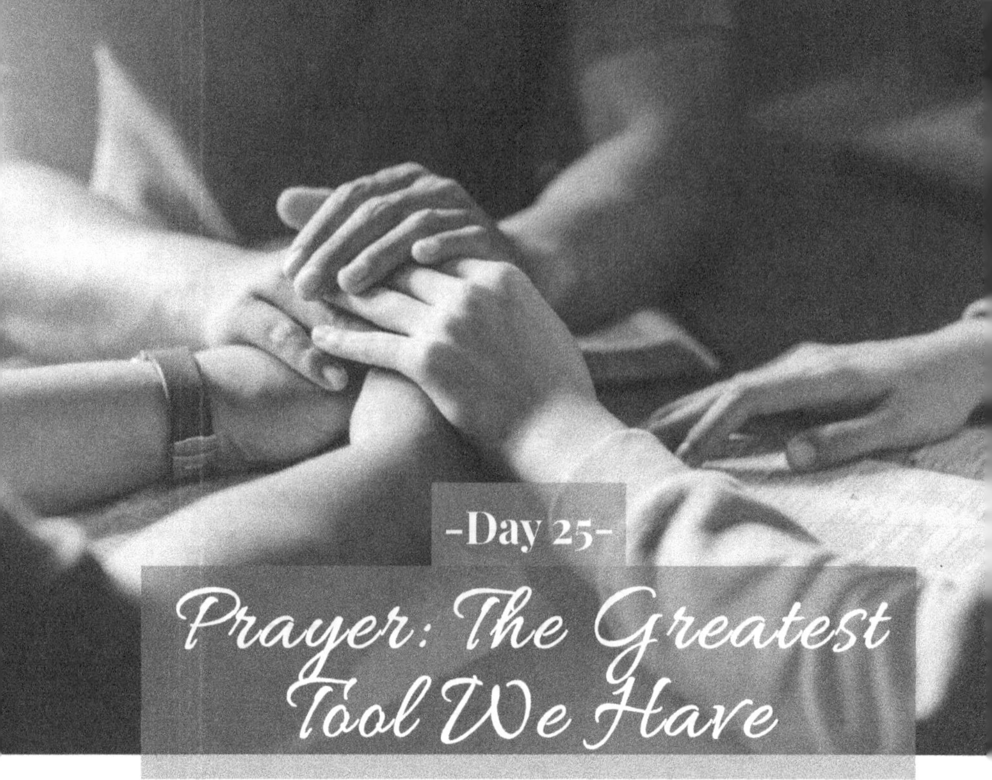

Prayer: The Greatest Tool We Have

The effective prayer of a righteous man can accomplish much.
—James 5:16

N o greater heartache occurs than when one of our children is suffering or experiencing a tough trial. One father knew all too well what this was like as he brought his demon-possessed child to Jesus.

> **When they came back to the disciples, they saw a large crowd around them, and some scribes arguing with them. Immediately, when the entire crowd saw Him, they were amazed and began running up to greet Him. And He asked them, "What are you discussing with them?" And one of the crowd answered Him, "Teacher, I brought You my son, possessed with a spirit which makes him mute; and whenever it seizes him, it slams him to the ground and he foams at the mouth, and grinds his**

> *teeth and stiffens out. I told Your disciples to cast*
> *it out, and they could not do it." And He answered*
> *them and said, "O unbelieving generation, how*
> *long shall I be with you? How long shall I put up*
> *with you? Bring him to Me!" They brought the boy*
> *to Him. When he saw Him, immediately the spirit*
> *threw him into a convulsion, and falling to the*
> *ground, he began rolling around and foaming at*
> *the mouth. And He asked his father, "How long has*
> *this been happening to him?" And he said, "From*
> *childhood. It has often thrown him both into the*
> *fire and into the water to destroy him. But if You*
> *can do anything, take pity on us and help us!"*
> *And Jesus said to him, "'If You can?' All things are*
> *possible to him who believes." Immediately the*
> *boy's father cried out and said, "I do believe; help*
> *my unbelief."*
> *(Mark 9:14-24)*

Desperate for help, the father said, "But if You can do anything, take pity on us and help us!" As Jesus heard his words, He responded by saying, "'If You can?' All things are possible to him who believes." The man immediately cried out and said, "I do believe; help my unbelief." So often our lives are like this story. We desperately need Jesus to act on our behalf, but we question if He really can. During one particular time in my life, I became so discouraged with my surroundings that my prayer life began to suffer. I was allowing what I could see (my circumstances) to shake my hope, instead of calling on my faith to allow God to strengthen me. After this revelation, everything began to change for the better.

> *For we walk by faith, not by sight.*
> *(2 Corinthians 5:7)*

The more time we spend in God's Word, getting to know Him, the more our faith will grow. And as it blossoms, our prayer life will take on an entirely different view. We will begin to pray from a place of hope instead of from a place of unbelief.

> ***And without faith it is impossible to please Him,***
> ***for he who comes to God must believe that He is***
> ***and that He is a rewarder of those who seek Him.***
> ***(Hebrews 11:6)***

From what place do you find yourself praying from today? Are you allowing the scene in front of you to speak louder to you than God's promises to you? Are you allowing the time you have been giving to this prayer request (which seems to have resulted in no change in sight) to cause you to shrink back in prayer? Or are you allowing unbelief to squander out your faith?

Prayer is one of the greatest tools we have. God loves to spend time not only listening to His children in prayer but also answering them as well. Wherever you find yourself today, do not stop praying. Keep seeking, keep knocking, and keep believing. For God will move on your behalf, according to His perfect will, in His perfect timing.

"I do believe; help my unbelief."

> ***Ask, and it will be given to you; seek, and you will***
> ***find; knock, and it will be opened to you.***
> ***(Matthew 7:7)***
>
> ***This is the confidence which we have before Him,***
> ***that, if we ask anything according to His will, He***
> ***hears us.***
> ***(1 John 5:14)***

Don't pray when you feel like it. Have an appointment with the Lord and keep it. A man is powerful on his knees.[3]

---

3.   Corrie ten Boom. Public domain.

Lord, please help me . . .

____

____

____

____

____

____

____

____

____

Lord, please help me . . .

____

____

Then Jesus answered and said, "Were there not ten cleansed? But the nine—where are they?"
—Luke 17:17

When I was growing up and attending my home church, on many occasions we would sing that old familiar hymn, "Count Your Many Blessings." The message it portrayed served as a reminder to not only "count those blessings" but name them, "one by one." Not only did the song promote the ongoing significance of recalling the blessings of God, it also prompted those listening to be thankful for such godsends.

Often times in prayer, if we are not careful, we may find ourselves placing more emphasis on our requests than we do on being thankful for all that God has done and continues to do in our lives (our good health, a place to live, our family, knowing Him as Lord and Savior, etc.). Regretfully, on more occasions than I can list, I would come desperate before God in prayer over what I wanted, yet I lacked greatly in spending time with Him in thanksgiving over His answers and even interventions.

As Jesus was passing between Samaria and Galilee, He encountered ten lepers, crying out to Him for help. The Savior wasted no time healing the individuals in need, for He loves His creation. Yet soon after the miracle took place, something very intriguing caught the attention of Jesus.

> *While He was on the way to Jerusalem, He was passing between Samaria and Galilee. As He entered a village, ten leprous men who stood at a distance met Him; and they raised their voices, saying, "Jesus, Master, have mercy on us!" When He saw them, He said to them, "Go and show yourselves to the priests." And as they were going, they were cleansed. Now one of them, when he saw that he had been healed, turned back, glorifying God with a loud voice, and he fell on his face at His feet, giving thanks to Him. And he was a Samaritan. Then Jesus answered and said, "Were there not ten cleansed? But the nine—where are they? Was no one found who returned to give glory to God, except this foreigner?" And He said to him, "Stand up and go; your faith has made you well."*
> *(Luke 17:11-19)*

Even though the Lord healed ten lepers on this day, only one returned to offer thanks. Overtaken by the goodness of the Lord, the former leper glorified Jesus' name in gratitude for his healing. However, immediately following his moment of thankfulness, Jesus paused to ask the man a question: "Were there not ten cleansed? But the nine—where are they?"

The lepers uttered desperate cries toward Jesus in hopes of a miracle. Yet the minute Jesus granted the request, nine of them continued on their way, without any regard to the Savior who had restored the men to good health.

Jesus tells us in all things to give thanks.

> *In everything give thanks; for this is God's will for you in Christ Jesus.*
> *(1 Thessalonians 5:18)*
>
> *Let the peace of Christ rule in your hearts, to which indeed you were called in one body; and be thankful.*
> *(Colossians 3:15)*
>
> *Whatever you do in word or deed, do all in the name of the Lord Jesus, giving thanks through Him to God the Father.*
> *(Colossians 3:17)*
>
> *Be anxious for nothing, but in everything by prayer and supplication with thanksgiving let your requests be made known to God.*
> *(Philippians 4:6)*

Take a few minutes today and just spend time thanking God for all that He has done for your life. Count those many blessings to Him, giving thanks for each one. Spend time worshipping your great Savior, who hears your pleas and who intervenes in ways that astound you to this day.

God is worthy of our praise and our thanksgivings. Thank Him for all that He has done and continues to do.

Lord, please help me . . .

The sacrifices of God are a broken spirit;
A broken and a contrite heart, O God, You will not despise.
—Psalm 51:17

At times we may find ourselves in a struggle over where God is leading us or the plan He has unfolded for our lives. This was the case with me during a particular season as I battled with uncertainties, while grappling to understand both God's direction as well as the waiting room to which He had called me. I became anxious, allowing fear to guide me. But what culminated from this trial was an intervention from God through a period of intense brokenness, where His comfort overruled my fear, and where I gleaned many great lessons from a loving Savior.

Days had quickly turned into weeks, and before I knew it, months would ensue with unresolved fear and worry. From within, a conflict was evolving, thus affecting my worship. I prayed to God to break whatever barrier was within me. Little did I know the answer would be revealed the very next day.

It was 5 a.m. when I awoke from my sleep. The enemy was attacking my faith like never before. I began to pace the floor, quoting scripture one minute while doubting my faith the next. However, unbeknownst to me, God Himself was about to conquer a battle that had raged in my soul for months.

In the next room from where I was sleeping stood my mother's library. Rows of bookshelves lined the walls, with Bibles, commentaries, and encouraging truths to comfort wounded souls. Hanging from those shelves were the most amazing visuals. My mother had taped handwritten scripture passages on many of the ridges. Those verses would soon be used to calm a hurting heart.

On this particular morning, my mother was engaging in her daily routine, sitting in her library, bathing her soul in the Word of God. I had no intention of saying a word about my distress; I just needed company. Yet the minute I walked into her library, she looked at me and uttered, "What's wrong?" As soon as I heard those words, I went to the floor on my knees, sobbing uncontrollably.

A once-balanced life was now in question. Where was God leading me? What path was I to walk down? And if I were to be honest, the matter that pierced my soul the most was, *God, where are You?*

The enemy's mission in the trial? To use it to try and tempt us into doubting God's faithfulness or even His presence in the situation.

My mother refrained to offer counsel, yet instead she immediately began to pray. The more she called out to God, the harder I cried. Consequently, loads of sadness overwhelmed my soul. However, the barrier needing breaking was nothing more than my own will.

After a time, I arose from the floor and walked into the adjoining room, only to fall into my mother's bed. Tears continued to flow as I heard her begin reading the scriptures she had pasted on her bookshelves. As she quoted the passages, she would stop and pray, and then continue the scripture regime. Several verses calmed my heart—one being Psalm 143:8:

> ***Let me hear Your lovingkindness in the morning;***
> ***For I trust in You;***
> ***Teach me the way in which I should walk;***
> ***For to You I lift up my soul.***

In a matter of moments, my mother's voice began fading in and out. The Lord was gently putting my body back to sleep, while setting my soul to a complete rest. From brokenness came a peace and calmness that only God could bring.

Later as I awoke once more, I had the desire to read the entire Psalm of David from which my mother had quoted earlier. To say the least, I was amazed at how a man after God's own heart had struggled in similar ways as I had.

Just like David, we all have our moments when life seems to hit us hard. Questions fill our minds while doubts engage our hearts. Yet God understands these periods and stands ready to flood our souls with His love, grace, and truth. He is only a prayer away. Quoted by David, one of my favorite passages of scripture derives from another part of the psalm. It states,

> ***I would have despaired unless I had believed that I***
> ***would see the goodness of the LORD***
> ***In the land of the living.***
> ***(Psalm 27:13)***

While David struggled with mixed emotions, begging to control his life, He made a decision to believe in God's faithfulness. In other words, David trusted his Lord while refusing to be shaped or influenced by his trial.

No matter what we are facing or will face in days to come, our God is faithful. He will never leave us nor forsake us. Even though the path we are on may be difficult, God has a purpose for the course as well as for the traveler. Are you currently searching for God's will? Do you find yourself in a waiting period? If so, I want to leave you with the following passage.

> *Wait for the LORD;*
> *Be strong and let your heart take courage;*
> *Yes, wait for the LORD.*
> *(Psalm 27:14)*

Do not lose heart, my friend. Believe, just as David did, and the many that have come after him, that you will see the goodness of the Lord in the land of the living. Take courage.

Lord, please help me . . .

____

____

____

____

____

____

____

____

Throwing aside his cloak, he jumped up and came to Jesus. And answering him, Jesus said, "What do you want Me to do for you?" And the blind man said to Him, "Rabboni, I want to regain my sight!"
—Mark 10:50-51

After years of recurring knee pain, I finally surrendered to the notion that it was time for a full knee replacement. As the date of the surgery approached, people came together to take care of me in so many ways. One lady opened her home, cooked for me, and ministered to me for days. Others brought gifts and food, came for visits, ran errands, took me to the doctor/hospital, called, texted, and prayed for me. I was so blessed!

After a period of time, Patty, a friend and one of the board members for Entrusted Hope Ministries, walked into my Sunday school class to let me know she wanted to stop by my apartment and bring me lunch. Later in the week, she reached out to ask what I would like to eat. I said a salad would be fine. Days later when I heard a knock at my door, I knew Patty had arrived. I was excited to have company, and the thought of a good salad had my appetite stirring. However, when I opened the door to welcome Patty into my home, what I saw in her arms caught me off guard. Not only was she holding the one thing I requested, but she had filled both her arms with so much more.

Patty walked in holding a large box filled with an array of already-prepared food items. The box held enough food to last for days. Along with a gift card for yet more food, on top of the box was a pretty vase filled with beautiful white roses and flowers. Her incredible kindness touched me so much.

Patty and I had a wonderful visit, and then it was time for her to leave for an upcoming football game. I thanked her again for her gifts and her kindness and then walked her to the door. After her departure, I began to ponder over the spiritual lesson Patty had just taught right before my eyes. I thought about how Jesus longs to do more in our lives than we could ever hope for or imagine.

> ***Now to Him who is able to do far more abundantly beyond all that we ask or think, according to the power that works within us, to Him be the glory in the church and in Christ Jesus to all generations forever and ever. Amen.***
> ***(Ephesians 3:20-21)***

In Mark 10:46-52, we read the story of Bartimaeus and Jesus. Bartimaeus was a blind beggar who was sitting by the road, begging. When he heard Jesus was passing by, he cried out to Him for help. Jesus posed a question: "What do you want Me to do for you?" Bartimaeus's deep desire was to regain his sight. At this point in Bartimaeus's life, he did not ask for a few needs but rather for what he genuinely wanted, and Jesus gave it to him.

We can learn many lessons from Bartimaeus's life.

1. *Bartimaeus was a beggar:* To Bartimaeus, it was just another day of sitting on the side of the road, begging. He could not

see; therefore, he required the help of others. Little did he know that on this day, not only would Jesus pass by where he was sitting, but He would also intervene to provide for Bartimaeus's most desperate need.

2. *Bartimaeus cries out:* When Bartimaeus heard that Jesus was passing by, he began to cry out to Him. People attempted to quiet him, but he continued to cry out all the more. Finally, his persistent cries got the attention of Jesus.

3. *Jesus calls for Bartimaeus:* Jesus stated, "Call him *here.*" While others had only seen Bartimaeus as the blind beggar, Jesus saw what he would become after His intervention. While others were telling him to be quiet, Jesus stated, "Call him *here.*" Though others did not wish to speak with him, Jesus not only wanted to talk with him (the salad), but He also wanted to do abundantly more (the tray of food and goodies). The disciples told Bartimaeus, "Take courage, stand up! He is calling for you."

4. *Bartimaeus immediately comes to Jesus:* "Throwing aside his cloak, he jumped up and came to Jesus." Bartimaeus did not linger in coming to Jesus. Jesus saw, heard, and summoned him. Therefore, Bartimaeus "jumped up" and came to Jesus.

5. *Jesus poses a question, and Bartimaeus answers honestly:* To be honest, times in my life have occurred when I prayed like a beggar instead of like a child of the King. I would share with Jesus a few needs, while the one thing I most desperately wanted Him to do for me remained tucked away in my heart. Jesus stated to Bartimaeus, "What do you want Me to do for you?" Bartimaeus answered, "Rabboni, I want to regain my sight!"

6. *There is a "go" waiting for you:* The story of Bartimaeus and Jesus is a powerful one, but we must not overlook the ending. Jesus gave Bartimaeus what he wanted, and in doing so, He issued a "go" for him. He no longer had to sit as a beggar—he could now follow Jesus as a healed individual. He no longer had to yearn for what he wanted now because Jesus gave him exactly what he desired. He

could go forward in both joy and peace on a new path and a new journey. Much awaited Bartimaeus. Jesus said to him, "Go; your faith has made you well." *Immediately* he regained his sight and *began* following Him on the road.

We will always be thankful for the salads in our lives, but Jesus longs to give us more. A tray of goodies is waiting for you—arms full of blessings. What would you say if Jesus were to ask you today, "What do you want Me to do for you?"

Lord, please help me . . .

____

____

____

____

____

____

____

____

Even if You Let Go of Me, I Will Not Let Go of You

Be strong and courageous, do not be afraid or tremble at them,
for the LORD your God is the one who goes with you. He will not fail
you or forsake you.
—Deuteronomy 31:6

As I sat quietly in the distance, I watched with anticipation a little boy holding tightly to his dad. "Are you ready?" the father would say to his son. In the shallow end of the swimming pool, the father was attempting to teach his child how to swim for the very first time. The youngster was excited about the new adventure yet a little apprehensive about all it included.

The daddy's plan for instructing his son involved holding on to him as he swam. Still, the little boy was afraid of letting go. "Do you trust me?" asked the daddy to his son. "I trust you," said the boy. Then, out of the mouth of the dad came one phrase that gripped my heart most profoundly: "Even if you let go of me," said the dad, "I will not let go of you."

At times in life, God ushers us into new seasons—adjacent with ordained processes that at first may appear a little frightening. God may call us to step out of our comfort boats to march on new waters or summon us to pull up our anchors that keep us tied to a solace dock. Why? It is so that we can swim out with the Lord into the deep waters of all that He has for our lives. Yet, oftentimes, when the moment arrives to step out or to let go, we may be tempted to shrink back due to fear.

> *Peter said to Him, "Lord, if it is You, command*
> *me to come to You on the water." And He*
> *said, "Come!" And Peter got out of the boat,*
> *and walked on the water and came toward*
> *Jesus. But seeing the wind, he became frightened,*
> *and beginning to sink, he cried out, "Lord, save*
> *me!" Immediately Jesus stretched out His hand*
> *and took hold of him, and said to him, "You of*
> *little faith, why did you doubt?" When they got*
> *into the boat, the wind stopped. And those who*
> *were in the boat worshiped Him, saying, "You are*
> *certainly God's Son!"*
> *(Matthew 14:28-33)*

God has promised us in His Word that He will never leave us nor forsake us. At times our circumstances may beg to differ, yet during such periods, we must remember that God is in control of our situations, and He is also in control of His children. He will not leave us to the winds of the storm or allow us to be overtaken by the torrential waters of trials. He will always reach out, take hold, and bring us to Him. He lives within us and surrounds us with His everlasting care and protection.

> *He who dwells in the shelter of the Most High*
> *Will abide in the shadow of the Almighty.*
> *I will say to the LORD, "My refuge and my fortress,*
> *My God, in whom I trust!"*

> *For it is He who delivers you from the snare of the*
> *trapper*
> *And from the deadly pestilence.*
> *He will cover you with His pinions,*
> *And under His wings you may seek refuge;*
> *His faithfulness is a shield and bulwark.*
> *You will not be afraid of the terror by night,*
> *Or of the arrow that flies by day;*
> *Of the pestilence that stalks in darkness,*
> *Or of the destruction that lays waste at noon.*
> *A thousand may fall at your side*
> *And ten thousand at your right hand,*
> *But it shall not approach you.*
> *You will only look on with your eyes*
> *And see the recompense of the wicked.*
> *For you have made the LORD, my refuge,*
> *Even the Most High, your dwelling place.*
> *No evil will befall you,*
> *Nor will any plague come near your tent.*
> *For He will give His angels charge concerning you,*
> *To guard you in all your ways.*
> *They will bear you up in their hands,*
> *That you do not strike your foot against a stone.*
> *(Psalm 91:1-12)*

As Christians, we will always hear the same words from our heavenly Father, just as the child heard from his earthly one during his time of learning how to swim: "Do you trust, Me?"

God always sees the bigger picture. No matter the boats He beckons us to "step out of," or the docks He bids us to "let go of," we can know with certainty He will be faithful to His own, never letting go even when we falter. Do not miss the opportunity to obey the Lord's calling for your life. A great gulf of blessings is waiting for you to swim out to in faith. He will never let go of you.

Lord, please help me . . .

They said to Him, "Teacher, this woman has been caught in adultery, in the very act. Now in the Law Moses commanded us to stone such women; what then do You say?"
—John 8:4-5

S andy was a young lady who had given her life over to Christ and was living for Him in mighty ways. However, she often faced questions about her past from family members and individual acquaintances. Repeatedly Sandy encountered people who mentioned issues from her yesterdays. Before long, Sandy was allowing the treatment from others to have an extreme impact on the way she was viewing the Lord's forgiveness of her past.

One day, a woman named Norma took Sandy under her wing to mentor. As the Holy Spirit began to work in Sandy's heart, a newfound freedom began to emerge. Sandy eventually came to the realization that even though others were choosing to live in her history, she no longer had to live there. Sandy experienced an even greater liberty from people's judgement—not only of her past but of what they deemed her future to be. The only opinion that mattered to Sandy was that of the Lord.

I knew my sin had caused both hurt and disappointment in people's lives. I also knew that through God's leading, I had a responsibility to make it right with the Lord first and then with those whom my sin had affected. As God led me in this process, I experienced His presence and peace as well as the forgiveness of others.

Yet one of the most profound, life-changing lessons took place when God moved my spirit to respond to what He had to say about my life. No matter how others viewed me, God was calling my heart to comply with His opinion and His alone. I remember sitting in the middle of my den in Birmingham, Alabama, reading an account of a woman caught in the act of adultery. A group of men brought her to Jesus, prompting a dialogue that included the following: (a) they exposed her sin, (b) they offered advice of what should be done as related to her sin, and (c) they posed a question that would leave the matter completely up to Jesus. The question: "What then do You say?"

> *But Jesus went to the Mount of Olives. Early in the morning He came again into the temple, and all the people were coming to Him; and He sat down and began to teach them. The scribes and the Pharisees brought a woman caught in adultery, and having set her in the center of the court, they said to Him, "Teacher, this woman has been caught in adultery, in the very act. Now in the Law Moses commanded us to stone such women; what then do You say?"*
> *(John 8:1-5)*

Jesus' reply not only shocked the woman but caused the men to look at their own lives as well. He stated, "He who is without sin among you, let him be the first to throw a stone at her." At his response, the stone throwers walked away one by one.

My heart became captivated by the moment in which Jesus was alone with the woman (John 8:9). I can just see her now, broken, ashamed, and afraid. Yet she stayed with Jesus. I believe something inside of her knew the man staring at her was an individual who loved and cared for her soul and for her well-being, so instead of running, she remained.

As Jesus looked at the woman, he made it clear the Pharisees no longer condemned her, nor did He condemn her. He then instructed her to go and sin no more.

Out of many, I would like to bring forth two things from this story that apply to anyone who has a past and has repented of it:

1. Some people in your life may desire to expose your sin in front of others for their own personal gain. If this happens, we must let God avenge His own. Do not allow yourself to get entangled with individuals trying to cause hurt. God will take care of you.
2. Some people along the way may continue to talk about your mistakes, refusing to believe you have changed. If this happens, I want to encourage you to refrain from making it your mission to defend yourself. Your living for Christ will be your defense. You never have to say a word.

> *Though I walk in the midst of trouble, You will revive me;*
> *You will stretch forth Your hand against the wrath of my enemies,*
> *And Your right hand will save me.*
> *The LORD will accomplish what concerns me;*
> *Your lovingkindness, O LORD, is everlasting;*
> *Do not forsake the works of Your hands.*
> *(Psalm 138:7-8)*

Today, we are surrounded by Pharisees who are always focusing on other people's faults instead of on their own. If we do not guard our hearts, we can start believing what the Pharisees of our lives think of us and then lean toward imagining that God maintains the same thoughts. Our hearts can become ensnared when we start trusting in man's opinion over that of God's. When people come against you or doubt God's desire to use your life, you, too, can pose the question, "What then do You say, Lord?" God's answer is what matters the most.

Lord, please help me . . .

____

____

____

____

____

____

____

____

____

____

More from Dr. O'Shea Lowery
& Innovo Publishing

My Life as a Single Mom
Seven Biblical Lessons for Transforming Your Life and Family

God created you with a unique purpose and plan.

My Life as a Single Mom: Seven Biblical Lessons for Transforming Your Life and Family is a seven-week individual study composed of collective works from God's Word and from others who lived centuries before. This study is geared toward single mothers but is an essential resource for all women, addressing fundamental truths every woman needs to walk in her faith. Through His Word, God gives principles to instruct her, wisdom to guide her, and truths to help her as she moves forward on the journey that has been entrusted to her.

Going Deeper
A Discipleship Model on the Gospel of Luke
LEADER'S GUIDE & STUDENT WORKBOOK

What does it look like to live out the Great Commission?

Going Deeper is a discipleship model on the Gospel of Luke intended for weekly small group gatherings. Groups will dive into the Word of God together, hold each other accountable, pray for one another, and live life together. Encouraging a mutual commitment to one another, the Student Workbook and the Leader's Guide edition work hand in hand to provide a comprehensive study on this book of the Bible. There is no greater investment one can make than to join together and point each other to Jesus. Going Deeper does just that.